MARTHA STEWART'S
PRESSURE COOKER

MARTHA STEWART'S
PRESSURE COOKER

100+ FABULOUS NEW RECIPES FOR THE PRESSURE COOKER, MULTICOOKER, AND INSTANT POT®

FROM THE EDITORS OF MARTHA STEWART LIVING
PHOTOGRAPHS BY MARCUS NILSSON

Clarkson Potter/Publishers
New York

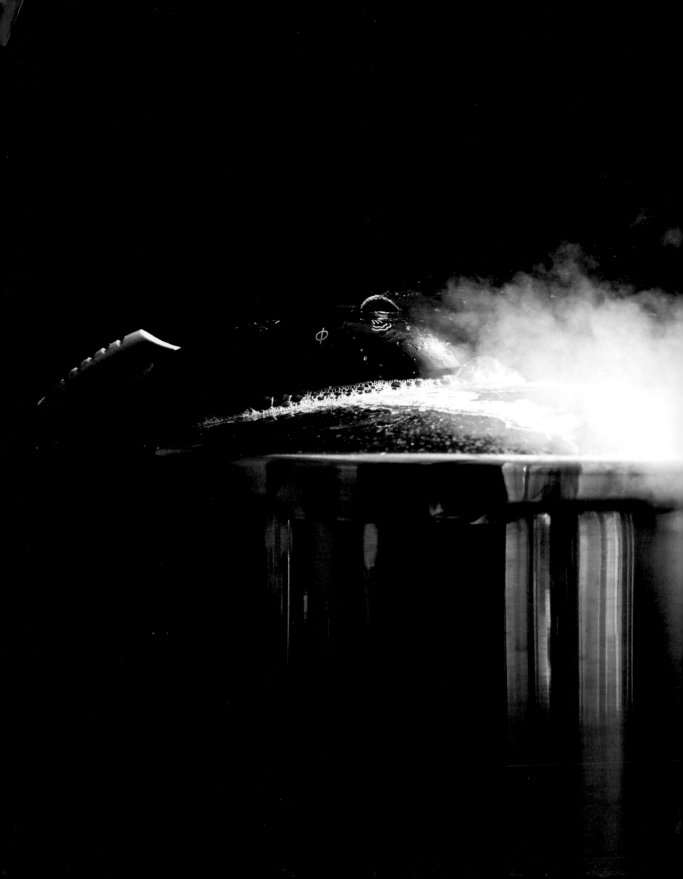

*To all those mothers who taught us how to use
the pressure cooker way back when*

CONTENTS

INTRODUCTION

In the past couple of years, we have created three books on single-subject cooking: *One Pot*, *Slow Cooker*, and now *Pressure Cooker*. There is widespread interest in recipes using these efficient, time-saving, modern cooking vessels, despite the fact that they use techniques that have been around for many years and have inspired more than just a few cookbooks. Our books approach these vessels very differently, taking full advantage of the improved technology used to build the new slow cookers and the once "scary to use" pressure cookers, enabling us to cook safely, fearlessly, quickly, and practically. We had you, the reader, in mind as we developed and tested all of these recipes, knowing very well that you are pressed for time, often cooking on a budget, and hoping to make nutritious and flavorful meals for yourself and your family in an unfussy but interesting way.

As in our mothers' day, some foods are just natural fits for pressure-cooking: dried beans, rice, economy cuts of meat, and dense vegetables like squash, turnips, and beets. Yet we have greatly expanded the range of foods that one can cook comfortably and deliciously in the pressure cooker to include risotto, international stews, soups, and chowders, and other vegetables that generally require long cooking times, like artichokes and leeks. Tamales, noodles, and curries are all treated to new interpretations, resulting in mouthwatering dishes. Even amazing desserts—ten of them—are represented with unique and excellent recipes that are sure to enter your personal repertoire of sweet endings to your meals.

We urge you to read about pressure-cooking and its benefits first, and then to try the recipes. We are very sure you will adapt quickly and effortlessly to the ease with which a dish can be prepared using the time-tested but newly improved pressure cooker.

Martha Stewart

PRESSURE COOKER BASICS

The pressure cooker is aptly named—in two ways. First, the ingenious airtight pot relies on a marked increase in pressure to significantly cut down on cooking times. Second, it decreases the *pressure* on you, the home cook, to put together a tasty meal from scratch, quickly and efficiently. There's no need to start prepping meals hours in advance or spend long stretches hovering over a simmering pot, spoon in hand. In the pressure cooker, lamb shanks turn falling-off-the-bone tender in less than half an hour, and making risotto—a process that traditionally involves constant stirring over low heat—is entirely hands off. The concentrated steam of the cooker, rather than your own elbow grease, helps the meat, grains, or vegetables reach the perfect state of done and delicious.

There's a lot more to pressure-cooking than the convenience, however. This method also delivers serious dishes with superior texture. High pressure extracts more flavor and gelatin from chicken or beef bones, for example, resulting in richer, fuller-bodied stocks. Cooking beans under high pressure eliminates the need for presoaking and results in a creamier texture. (It's no surprise that the pressure cooker is considered a kitchen essential in legume-loving countries like India and Nepal.) Because the pot is sealed airtight, precious moisture and flavoring agents can't escape, which adds up to juicier pork shoulder, umami-packed short ribs, and gorgeously fragrant lamb curry.

So why isn't the pressure cooker more of a staple in American kitchens? The answer lies in that story you probably heard about your grandmother's old-school cooker with the weighted pressure regulator spewing soup all over her ceiling—and causing her to swear off pressure-cooking for life. Scary accidents like that branded the cooker as dangerous, but these days its bad rap is thoroughly unwarranted. Modern pressure cookers are safe, armed with multiple backup features that allow excess pressure to escape long before building up to explosive proportions. And that's not the only reason these pots are making a comeback. Many of these new-generation cookers, such as the wildly popular Instant Pot, are practically one-stop tools—they can also be used as slow cookers, rice pots, and yogurt makers. Perhaps most important, these fast, multifunctional gadgets are nearly foolproof.

Pressure-cooking can lead to substantial savings at the supermarket, too: Once you realize that the base of a deeply delicious chicken soup can be produced from leftover bones in less time than it takes to go food shopping, you may never be tempted to buy canned or boxed stock again. In just an hour or so on a Sunday night, you can pressure-cook a host of building blocks for the week of meals ahead: batches of beans, pots of grains, quarts of soup. You can make the most of some of the more inexpensive cuts of meat at the supermarket, too, transforming them into tender pieces in less than an hour. Start cooking your way through the recipes in this book, each of which includes directions for both stovetop and electric models, and you'll quickly see what all the fuss is about—this humble pot truly is the ultimate shortcut.

GET TO KNOW
YOUR PRESSURE COOKER

Believe it or not, the pressure cooker was invented way back in the seventeenth century, by French physicist Denis Papin. The first saucepan-style pressure cookers aimed at home cooks weren't introduced until the twentieth century, however, when they debuted at the 1939 New York World's Fair under the brand name Presto. The cookers soon became immensely popular, especially during World War II, when women, having stepped into the workforce in greater numbers, began looking for faster ways to feed their families. The original models, while handy, were also tricky: If one neglected to turn the heat down once the pot reached high pressure, the pressure would continue to build until the cooker literally popped its top, resulting in, at best, a mess, and, at worst, some serious burns. It's no wonder, then, that when convenience foods like TV dinners flooded the market in the 1950s, many women traded their pressure cookers for freezers and, a couple of decades later, microwaves.

It wasn't until the 1990s that second generation pressure cookers emerged, complete with a variety of backup safety vents that permitted excess pressure to escape well before reaching dangerous levels. And in the years since that initial leap forward, pressure cookers have continued to evolve in terms of safety and functionality, with auto-lock lids, at-a-glance pressure indicators, and even high-tech features like digital display screens and wireless connectivity.

The pressure cookers available on the market today can be divided into two main types: electric and stovetop. Both work on the same general principle: You lock the lid into place (the cookers have a safety feature that requires the lock be in place before the pressure can rise), add the ingredients, and heat the cooker until the liquid comes to a boil, producing steam. The steam is trapped inside the sealed pot, forcing pressure to build. When the cooker is operating at high pressure, water boils at about 250 rather than 212 degrees, breaking down fibers of tough cuts of meat, for example, and marrying flavors at two to three times faster speeds than traditional stovetop- or oven cooking methods.

With electric models, you just add ingredients, lock the lid into place, and push a few buttons to seal the pot and set the timer. When the timer runs out, the heating element turns off, allowing the pressure to drop naturally as the cooker cools. The pressure can also be released more quickly by opening a valve to release steam. Most newer models include a "keep warm" setting that will hold food at serving temperature for several hours and a "sauté" feature with multiple temperature settings to let you gently soften aromatic vegetables, give meat a good sear, or reduce cooking liquid to form a sauce. With older-model electric cookers, those tasks had to be performed in a separate pan on the stove—which, of course, meant another dirty dish to clean.

These added capabilities offer considerable advantages. Our test kitchen found that often the difference between a passable recipe and a truly delicious one was that bit of extra care taken before or after the pressure-cooking itself (but also in the machine). Sautéing the onions, ginger, and spices deepens the complexity of the Lamb and Potato Curry (page 162), for example. Searing the beef amps up the taste of Pot Roast with Dates, Olives, and Orange (page 153). And a quick simmer at the end allows the fish in the Salmon Chowder (page 165) to cook to tender perfection.

As advanced as the new electric models may be, stovetop cookers offer more control over such steps. Because you're cooking over a burner rather than relying on a preset electric heat source, you can modulate the temperature more quickly and more evenly, and you can attain a better sear. Stovetop pots, however, require more attention once pressure-cooking gets under way. After locking the lid, you place the cooker over high heat and then must monitor it closely until the desired level of pressure is achieved, at which point you lower the heat just enough to retain pressure. If you wait too long to turn down the heat, your food can quickly scorch. (Some cooks, when using older electric stoves with burners that take time to heat up or cool down, use two burners for this process, setting one to high heat and a second to low, and moving the cooker from one burner to the other once pressure is achieved.) For the duration of cooking time, you have to keep an eye on the pot, turning up the heat if the pressure begins to wane. As with the electric pressure cooker, the pressure can be released either quickly, by venting steam, or naturally, by allowing the temperature to drop. Most of the recipes in this book call for quick release, as we found it adds a greater element of control over the cooking; with natural release, expect the food to continue to cook while the temperature drops.

Modern pressure cookers feature a spring-valve pressure regulator, making it easy to tell when the pot has come to pressure: a brightly colored rod rises until it reaches a designated mark. Some models have marks for both high and low pressure, but the low-pressure setting, which exerts about half as much pressure per square inch as the high setting, is used sparingly, when gentler cooking is required—for instance, with eggs. (All the recipes in this book call for high pressure.)

As well as offering more control, stovetop models have some other advantages over their high-tech cousins: Electric cookers generally take longer to come to pressure and often exert a bit less pressure on food, resulting in slightly longer cooking times. Electric pressure cookers also cost more than stovetop models and are usually bigger, and thus harder to store. But because many of the new models are often multifunctional, doing away with the need for a slow cooker and a rice pot, many cooks don't mind the extra bulk or the higher price tag. The biggest advantage, of course, is that they are easy to use—push a few buttons and you're set. (Many cookers offer preset cooking times for specific foods; we like the extra level of control that comes with using manually set cook times. Your cooker may have a button that says "Manual" or simply "Pressure Cook.") Ultimately, the model you choose depends on your own needs, so keep the pros and cons in mind and decide what works best for you, your family, and your kitchen space.

So-called **JIGGLE-TOP** pressure cookers—the type your grandmother may have used—have a small weight that sits atop the vent pipe, instead of the spring-valve pressure regulator used in contemporary cookers. When those old-school cookers come to pressure, the weight begins to rock back and forth, signaling the cook to turn down the heat. Although jiggle-top pressure cookers can be safe, provided they include venting features, we prefer spring-valve models and advocate their use. They are not only easier to operate but also much quieter. The sound emitted by jiggle-top cookers has often been compared to a small freight train.

THE PRESSURE PRINCIPLES

Whether you choose a high-tech multiuse appliance or a basic stovetop version, mastering pressure-cooking requires a bit of practice, involving at least a few trials (and the occasional error). Here is our recipe developers' best advice for making the most of your machine—and avoiding the most common pitfalls.

1. THINK BIG

For the sake of storage, it might be tempting to seek out a petite pressure cooker—after all, cookers come as small as three quarts. But the recipes in this book are designed for six- to eight-quart models, and we don't recommend going any smaller. Because the pots should be only partially filled for safety reasons, a tiny cooker doesn't make much practical sense.

2. BE PREPARED

After purchasing any new kitchen gadget, it's hard to resist the urge to run home and start playing with it immediately, barely glancing at the manual in the process. But in this case, a study of the instructions is especially crucial. Every cooker works differently, and if you're not familiar with the ins and outs of your machine before you start using it, you're more likely to end up with scorched food and spent patience.

3. TEST THE WATERS

A great way to get familiar with your pressure cooker is to take it for a trial run with four cups of plain water. This simple introduction will offer hands-on experience with the machine's features without the risk of ruining dinner. And by measuring the water before and after, you'll be able to determine how much evaporation occurs during cooking. Some pots lose no water at all, while others lose a considerable amount. The recipes on the following pages provide a range for water, to accommodate both stovetop (which generally requires more water) and electric pressure cookers.

4. BEGIN WITH BEANS

Once you've taken your pot through a not-so-dry run with water, you're ready to start pressure-cooking in earnest. We recommend beginning with a batch of beans. They will allow you to familiarize yourself with the machine, without a lot of expense. (In other words, if you have to start over, it's not the end of the world.) Keep in mind that beans cook differently, depending on type, size, and age. So if your pintos or garbanzos turn out tough, just continue to simmer them. One thing to note: Our recipe developers found that beans had the best texture when they were allowed to rest in their cooking liquid for an additional thirty minutes after venting pressure and removing the lid.

5. CUT TO SIZE

Those who know their way around the kitchen recognize the importance of chopping ingredients into similarly sized pieces so they cook at the same rate. When that rate is accelerated, as with pressure-cooking, uniformity is all the more important. Also, avoid chopping vegetables too small or too large. A too-small morsel can very quickly turn to mush, while an overly large piece might emerge tough or undercooked.

6. DON'T OVERFILL

A packed-to-the-brim pressure cooker will spill over quite dramatically when pressure is released. In these situations, food particles also tend to escape through the steam vent, causing clogs. A good rule of thumb is to fill the pot to a maximum of one-half capacity for ingredients with a tendency to produce foam and two-thirds capacity for everything else. With beans, we found that adding a tablespoon of oil to the cooking water cut down on foaming. Even so, when cooking a potentially foamy ingredient (think oatmeal and just about any other grain, as well as beans), it's smart to lightly cover the vent with a clean kitchen towel when releasing steam, to avoid a mess.

7. ACCESSORIZE

Inexpensive add-ons like steaming baskets, racks, ramekins, and cake pans can greatly increase your cooker's utility. Many models come with a few accessories. Others you probably already own—it's not necessary that they be designed expressly for pressure-cooking, as long as they're heatproof and fit comfortably inside your pot (this means 7-inch cake pans, for example).

You can even create your own foil sling, a tool that proves very useful when lifting a cooked dish, like the flan on page 229, out of the pressure cooker. (We use it in this book primarily for desserts.) To make a sling: Fold one 20-inch length of aluminum foil lengthwise in three. Place the pan over the foil sling and transfer to the pressure cooker, holding the sling in place. Fold tops of the sling down, if necessary, to avoid interfering with the cooker's lid.

8. GET TOUGH

Think of the pressure cooker as the ultimate tenderizer. Where the machine truly excels is in transforming tough cuts of meat—think pork shoulder, brisket, and short ribs—into succulent dinners. The same logic holds for root vegetables and even dried beans. Many cooks prefer to prepare quick-simmering legumes, such as the lentils used in Indian dal, in a pressure cooker. While the cooker doesn't shave off much time in that case, it does deliver incomparable creaminess.

9. USE COMMON SENSE

Practically any food can be pressure-cooked, but sometimes doing so doesn't actually save time or improve flavor or texture. Tender, fast-cooking vegetables like fresh green beans or spinach can generally be sautéed or blanched more quickly and easily. The same can be said about delicate fish. And the pressure cooker just doesn't do crunchy—dishes like gratins and whole chickens are better cooked in a good old-fashioned oven, where they'll crisp up nicely.

10. SAFETY FIRST (AND LAST)

Though faulty cookers won't be an issue, there are a few simple safety tips to follow: After the pot comes to pressure, release the vent *away* from your hands and face, letting the hot steam escape. And when removing the lid, again open *away* from you. At this point, all pressure will have been released, but residual steam will escape. You can use a clean kitchen towel to release the steam vent or remove the lid, if you like. Keep the towel handy when cooking grains and beans (as noted above), to lightly cover the vent when releasing steam.

PART ONE

Building Blocks & Variations

The quickest and best way to master your pressure cooker is to begin with a few building blocks. Think of these as gateway recipes, primed for experimentation and improvisation once you start to understand how the machine works. These recipes utilize accessible, affordable ingredients—beans, grains, sturdy vegetables, and the components of good stock. Many of the recipes in this section were designed to serve as jumping-off points: Pressure-cook a batch of chickpeas, for example, then use them to prepare all manner of other dishes—a starter (say, Roasted-Red-Pepper Hummus on page 34), a side dish (Chickpea and Chorizo Salad on page 37), or a lunch or lighter dinner (Chickpea-Carrot Fritters on page 33). Once you've tried your hand at these simple dishes, you're ready to tackle all kinds of delicious main courses (see page 118) and desserts (see page 218)—made entirely in your pressure cooker.

CHICKEN STOCK

Making stock in the pressure cooker is a surefire way to fall in love with your machine. It takes less than an hour to produce rich, long-simmered flavor. Be sure to use all the water recommended (but no more) to get just the right amount of stock, then strain it twice after cooking for the smoothest consistency.

—————— **MAKES ABOUT 3 QUARTS** ——————

3 quarts water

3 pounds chicken wings, backs, or bones

1 large carrot, quartered

1 large celery stalk, quartered

1 large onion, quartered

2 large flat-leaf parsley sprigs

2 large thyme sprigs

1 dried bay leaf

½ teaspoon black peppercorns

1. Place all ingredients in a 6- to 8-quart pressure cooker.

2. **STOVETOP:** Secure lid. Bring to high pressure over medium-high heat; reduce heat to maintain pressure and cook for 30 minutes. Remove from heat, quickly release pressure, then remove lid.

   ELECTRIC: Secure lid. Manually set cooker to 30 minutes and let it come to pressure. Once time is complete, turn off, quickly release pressure, then remove lid.

3. Strain stock through a colander set over another pot (discard solids). Strain stock a second time through a fine-mesh sieve set over a large bowl. Skim any fat from surface. Let stock cool completely, uncovered. (Stock can be refrigerated in an airtight container up to 1 week, or frozen up to 6 months.)

You can use this **STOCK** for many recipes, including Butternut Squash Soup with Pistachio Oil (page 95), Pork and Pinto-Bean Chili (page 121), Coq au Vin (page 141), and Lamb and Potato Curry (page 162).

HAM STOCK

In the pressure cooker, a picnic ham (from the pork shoulder) not only becomes incredibly tender but also yields a versatile stock with smoky flavor to use as a base for soups, stews, noodle dishes, casseroles—anywhere you would ordinarily use chicken stock, in fact. Ham stock is saltier than most, so you may want to reduce the salt in specific recipes.

MAKES 6 TO 7 CUPS

1 smoked picnic ham
(about 3 pounds)

2½ quarts water

1. Place ham and the water in a 6- to 8-quart pressure cooker.

2. **STOVETOP:** Secure lid. Bring to high pressure over medium-high heat; reduce heat to maintain pressure and cook for 15 minutes. Remove from heat, quickly release pressure, then remove lid.

   ELECTRIC: Secure lid. Manually set cooker to 15 minutes and let it come to pressure. Once time is complete, turn off, quickly release pressure, then remove lid.

3. Skim any fat from surface. Let ham cool in liquid, uncovered. Transfer ham and stock into separate airtight containers and refrigerate until ready to use. (Stock can be refrigerated in an airtight container up to 1 week, or frozen up to 6 months.)

You can use this **STOCK** for Red Beans and Rice with Andouille (page 41), Molasses-Baked Beans with Bacon (page 57), Beet Soup with Sour Cream and Dill (page 93), and Wine-Braised Pork Shoulder (page 125). The **PICNIC HAM** can also be glazed in the oven, cubed for a salad, used in a breakfast strata, or sliced for sandwiches.

VEGETABLE STOCK

Homemade vegetable stock is fast, easy, inexpensive, and greatly superior to any store-bought version. We love the depth provided by concentrated tomato paste, sweet leek greens, and a generous amount of mushrooms. The flavors are rapidly extracted by the pressure cooker and retained once the liquid is strained. This stock is so nourishing that it may become your go-to when preparing soups and stews—even those made with meat or chicken.

MAKES ABOUT 3 QUARTS

3 quarts water

½ pound cremini mushrooms, trimmed and sliced

1 leek (green parts only), rinsed well

2 large carrots, trimmed and halved

1 large turnip, peeled and quartered

1 large celery stalk, halved

1 medium onion, quartered

1 bunch fresh flat-leaf parsley

4 thyme sprigs

3 dried bay leaves

1 tablespoon tomato paste

1 teaspoon black peppercorns

1½ teaspoons coarse salt

1. Place all ingredients in a 6- to 8-quart pressure cooker.

2. **STOVETOP:** Secure lid. Bring to high pressure over medium-high heat; reduce heat to maintain pressure and cook for 15 minutes. Remove from heat, quickly release pressure, then remove lid.

   ELECTRIC: Secure lid. Manually set cooker to 25 minutes and let it come to pressure. Once time is complete, turn off, quickly release pressure, then remove lid.

3. Strain stock through a fine-mesh sieve set over a large bowl (discard solids). Let stock cool completely, uncovered. (Stock can be refrigerated in an airtight container up to 1 week, or frozen up to 6 months.)

Use this **STOCK** for Potato Soup with All the Toppings (page 90), Beet Soup with Sour Cream and Dill (page 93), Minestrone (page 204), and Artichokes with Provençal Stuffing (page 216).

WHITE BEANS

BLACK BEANS

CHICKPEAS

FRENCH GREEN LENTILS

GIGANTE BEANS

RED BEANS

PRESSURE-COOKED BEANS & LEGUMES

If you cook nothing other than beans in your pressure cooker, it will still be well worth the investment. Where once there could be no spontaneity in preparing dishes that call for beans (other than canned), the cooker makes it quick and easy to have a batch at the ready in an hour or less (up to 30 minutes of cooking, followed by 30 minutes of tenderizing in the cooking liquid)—no presoaking required. Beans cook more consistently in the machine than on the stovetop—and the creamy texture is hard to beat.

There's a potential for foaming when cooking beans, so limit the level of ingredients and liquid to half the cooker's capacity and add a tablespoon of oil to the cooking water. As a further precaution, cover the vent with a clean kitchen towel when releasing the steam. This is good practice with food that tends to foam, like beans and grains.

For guidance on cooking times, follow the chart at right, keeping in mind that the beans' variety, age, and size can all affect the times. And before cooking legumes like lentils, sort through them to remove any stones and twigs.

MAKES ABOUT 6 CUPS

---

3 quarts water

1 pound dried beans or legumes (see chart at right)

1 tablespoon extra-virgin olive oil

1 teaspoon coarse salt

1. Place all ingredients in a 6- to 8-quart pressure cooker.

2. **STOVETOP:** Secure lid. Bring to high pressure over medium-high heat; reduce heat to maintain pressure and cook according to time provided for each type of bean. Remove from heat, quickly release pressure (loosely cover vent with a clean kitchen towel), then remove lid.

   ELECTRIC: Secure lid. Manually set cooker to time provided for each type of bean and let it come to pressure. Once time is complete, turn off, quickly release pressure (loosely cover vent with a clean kitchen towel), then remove lid.

3. Let beans stand in cooking liquid for 30 minutes; then drain. (Reserve cooking liquid.)

BEAN TYPE	STOVETOP PRESSURE COOKER	ELECTRIC PRESSURE COOKER
CHICKPEAS	25 MINUTES	30 MINUTES
RED BEANS	25 MINUTES	30 MINUTES
BLACK BEANS	20 MINUTES	25 MINUTES
WHITE BEANS	20 MINUTES	25 MINUTES
GIGANTE BEANS	15 MINUTES	15-18 MINUTES
FRENCH GREEN LENTILS	6 MINUTES	8 MINUTES

CHICKPEA-CARROT FRITTERS

Carrots add a touch of sweetness to these crisp fritters. Wrap them in a warm pita, add a dollop of lemon-yogurt dip, and you have a satisfying vegetarian main course. As an alternative topping, try herbed Greek yogurt or a schmear of labneh, the tangy, ultra-thick Middle Eastern yogurt. After preparing the chickpeas in the pressure cooker, save about a quarter-cup of the cooking liquid to add to the fritter batter to help bind the ingredients.

MAKES ABOUT 12 FRITTERS

2 cups cooked chickpeas (pages 30–31), plus ¼ cup cooking liquid

2 medium carrots, coarsely grated

1 large egg, lightly beaten

¼ cup all-purpose flour

1 teaspoon ground coriander

1 teaspoon chili powder

½ teaspoon baking powder

Coarse salt and freshly ground pepper

Extra-virgin olive oil, for frying

⅓ cup plain whole-milk yogurt or sour cream

⅓ cup mayonnaise

1 tablespoon fresh lemon juice

1. In a large bowl, coarsely mash chickpeas with a potato masher. Add reserved cooking liquid, carrots, egg, flour, coriander, chili powder, baking powder, 1½ teaspoons salt, and ½ teaspoon pepper; stir until combined.

2. Heat ¼ inch oil in a large skillet over medium. Working in batches, drop 6 mounds of batter (about 1½ tablespoons each) into skillet, then flatten gently with the back of a spoon. Cook, turning once, until golden brown, about 3 minutes per side. Transfer fritters to a paper-towel–lined plate.

3. In a small bowl, stir together yogurt, mayonnaise, lemon juice, and ½ teaspoon salt. Serve fritters with yogurt dip.

ROASTED-RED-PEPPER HUMMUS

Pressure-cooked chickpeas, together with roasted bell peppers and a bit of ground cayenne pepper for smoky heat, make for a truly exceptional hummus. We used raw tahini here, but for a more complex flavor, substitute roasted tahini. Serve with toasted pita, or other flatbread, sprinkled with coarse salt and fresh dill.

MAKES ABOUT 4 CUPS

2 red bell peppers

3 cups cooked chickpeas (pages 30–31), drained

¼ cup tahini

2 tablespoons extra-virgin olive oil, plus more for drizzling

2 tablespoons fresh lemon juice

1 garlic clove, minced

¼ teaspoon cayenne pepper

Coarse salt

Chopped fresh dill, for garnish

Toasted flatbread, for serving

1. Roast bell peppers over a gas flame, turning with tongs, until charred all over. (Alternatively, char under broiler, turning as needed.) Transfer to a bowl, cover, and let cool. Rub off skins with paper towels, using a knife to remove any stubborn spots. Remove and discard stems, ribs, and seeds. Cut bell peppers into strips.

2. Purée bell peppers, chickpeas, tahini, oil, lemon juice, garlic, cayenne, and 1¾ teaspoons salt in a food processor until desired smoothness is reached. Season with salt and drizzle with oil. Top with dill and serve with flatbread.

CHICKPEA AND CHORIZO SALAD

Bold Mediterranean ingredients like Spanish chorizo, the cured pork sausage with garlic and pimentón, push the pressure-cooked chickpea in a new direction in this lively salad. (Don't confuse Spanish chorizo with the Mexican variety, which is made from fresh pork and shouldn't serve as a substitute.)

SERVES 6 TO 8

¼ cup extra-virgin olive oil

½ pound Spanish chorizo, casings removed and sliced

1 small onion, halved and sliced

4 garlic cloves, smashed

2 tablespoons sherry vinegar

1 cup sliced pimiento-stuffed green olives

Cooked chickpeas (about 6 cups; pages 30–31), drained

2 ounces manchego cheese, shaved (about ½ cup)

½ cup packed fresh flat-leaf parsley, coarsely chopped

Coarse salt and freshly ground pepper

Heat oil in a large skillet over medium-high. Add chorizo and cook, stirring occasionally, until browned, about 5 minutes. With a slotted spoon, transfer chorizo to a paper-towel-lined plate. Add onion and garlic to skillet, and cook, stirring occasionally, until golden, about 6 minutes. Remove skillet from heat, and stir in vinegar and olives. Transfer to a serving bowl, and stir in reserved chorizo, chickpeas, cheese, and parsley. Season with salt and pepper, and serve.

FŪL MEDAMES

Dried fava beans are the traditional base for this warming stew, enjoyed in many variations throughout the Middle East and in parts of North Africa. But since favas are less readily available in the United States, even in their dried or canned forms, we made our fūl (as it is casually called) with red kidney beans, a fine substitute. In Egypt, fūl is most often eaten for breakfast with a fried or hard-cooked egg. You can follow that lead, or skip the egg and serve it as a substantial side dish.

SERVES 6 TO 8

¼ cup extra-virgin olive oil, plus more for drizzling

1 large onion, finely chopped

3 large garlic cloves, minced

1 teaspoon ground cumin

¼ teaspoon red-pepper flakes, plus more for serving

Cooked red kidney beans (about 6 cups; pages 30–31), drained

¼ cup fresh lemon juice

¼ cup coarsely chopped fresh flat-leaf parsley or cilantro

Coarse salt

Hot sauce, for serving

Heat oil in a medium pot over medium. Add onion and garlic, and cook, stirring, until softened, about 6 minutes. Add cumin and red-pepper flakes, and cook, stirring, until fragrant, about 1 minute. Add kidney beans and cook until heated through, about 5 minutes. Stir in lemon juice and parsley, and season with salt and red-pepper flakes. Drizzle with olive oil and serve with hot sauce.

RED BEANS AND RICE WITH ANDOUILLE

Although there's no one way to make this New Orleans staple (made even easier—and faster—in the pressure cooker), most versions include smoked meat; some prefer ham hocks, others turkey, with spicy andouille pork sausage the most beloved. The rice can be prepared either on the stovetop while the red beans are in the pressure cooker, or in the pressure cooker ahead of time. Serve with your favorite hot sauce and a cold beer.

SERVES 6 TO 8

¼ cup extra-virgin olive oil

1 pound andouille sausage or kielbasa, sliced ½ inch thick, or 1 pound ham, cut into ½-inch pieces, from making Ham Stock (page 25)

1 large onion, finely chopped

1 large celery stalk, finely chopped

1 small green bell pepper, ribs and seeds removed, finely chopped

3 large garlic cloves, minced

Cooked red kidney beans (about 6 cups; pages 30–31), plus 1 cup cooking liquid

1 cup Ham or Chicken Stock, homemade (page 25 or 24) or store-bought, or water

Coarse salt and freshly ground pepper

Cooked white rice (pages 66–67), for serving

Heat oil in a medium heavy pot or Dutch oven over medium. Add sausage and cook, stirring occasionally, until browned, about 8 minutes. With a slotted spoon, transfer sausage to a paper-towel–lined plate. Remove all but ¼ cup fat from pot and return over medium heat. Add onion, celery, bell pepper, and garlic, and cook, stirring, until softened, about 5 minutes. Add reserved sausage, kidney beans, reserved cooking liquid, stock, 1 teaspoon salt, and ½ teaspoon pepper. Cook, stirring occasionally, until liquid is absorbed, about 5 minutes. Serve over white rice.

RED-BEAN CHILI WITH CASHEWS

Spicy and smoky with roasted poblano peppers and canned chipotles in adobo, this vegetarian red-bean chili is balanced with the mild sweetness of cashews and grated carrot. This recipe is inspired by a favorite from the former Cabbagetown Café in Ithaca, New York.

SERVES 6 TO 8

2 poblano chiles or 2 cans (4.5 ounces each) chopped green chiles

¼ cup extra-virgin olive oil, plus more for pan

2 medium onions, finely chopped

3 garlic cloves, minced

1 tablespoon chili powder

1 teaspoon ground cumin

Coarse salt and freshly ground pepper

1 chipotle in adobo sauce, finely chopped, or more to taste

1 can (28 ounces) crushed tomatoes

Cooked red beans (about 6 cups; pages 30–31), plus 1 quart cooking liquid

2 large carrots, coarsely grated

2 cups (9 ounces) unsalted roasted cashews

Grated cheddar cheese, for serving

1. Preheat broiler to high. Cut poblanos in half lengthwise and remove ribs and seeds. Arrange poblanos on a lightly oiled baking sheet, cut sides down. Broil until blistered and charred, then transfer to a bowl and cover with plastic wrap to steam, 10 minutes. Remove skin and cut chiles into ¼-inch pieces.

2. Heat oil in a large pot over medium. Add onions and garlic, and cook, stirring, until softened, about 6 minutes. Add chili powder, cumin, and 1 teaspoon salt, and cook, stirring, 1 minute. Add poblanos, chipotle, tomatoes, reserved cooking liquid, carrots, and cashews, and bring to a boil. Reduce heat to medium and simmer, uncovered, until carrots are tender, about 10 minutes. Stir in beans, and season with salt and pepper. Serve topped with grated cheese.

BLACK BEAN AND GOAT CHEESE BURGERS

We combined pressure-cooked black beans with chopped onion, garlic, a few spices, cilantro, and soft goat cheese to create the *most* delicious vegetable burger. Refrigerate the black-bean mixture before shaping the patties so they hold their form, and keep the patties chilled until ready to cook. For gluten-free burgers, opt for rice flour over Wondra (a finely-ground instant flour), and serve with gluten-free rolls.

MAKES 10 BURGERS

¼ cup plus 3 tablespoons extra-virgin olive oil

1 medium onion, finely chopped

2 garlic cloves, minced

2 teaspoons ground cumin

1 teaspoon smoked paprika

Coarse salt

Cooked black beans (about 6 cups; pages 30–31), drained

6 ounces fresh goat cheese

½ cup fresh cilantro, finely chopped

1 cup rice flour or Wondra

Mashed avocado and alfalfa sprouts, for serving

Kaiser or gluten-free buns, toasted

1. Heat 3 tablespoons oil in a skillet over medium. Add onion and garlic, and cook, stirring occasionally, until golden brown, about 8 minutes. Add cumin, paprika, and 2 teaspoons salt, and cook, stirring, 1 minute. Add half the black beans and goat cheese, and mash with a potato masher or back of a large spoon; transfer to a large bowl. Stir in cilantro and remaining black beans and goat cheese until combined. Refrigerate black bean mixture, uncovered, until cold, at least 1 hour or up to 3 days.

2. Place rice flour in a wide shallow bowl. Form 10 patties (about ¾ inch thick), dredge in rice flour, then transfer to a baking sheet. Chill until firm, at least 1 hour or up to 1 day.

3. Heat remaining ¼ cup oil in a 12-inch nonstick skillet over medium-high until oil is shimmering, about 1 minute. Working in batches, cook burgers until golden and crisp, turning carefully, about 3 minutes per side (add more oil, if needed, between batches). Serve with mashed avocado, alfalfa sprouts, and buns.

You can prepare the **BURGER MIXTURE** (through Step 1) up to 3 days ahead.

BLACK BEAN, CUCUMBER, AND FETA SALAD

Earthy black beans meet cool cucumbers and bright cilantro, lime, and feta in this refreshing side dish that's ideal year-round. You can substitute diced fresh fennel for the cucumber—be sure to save the fronds for garnish.

SERVES 6 TO 8

Cooked black beans (about 6 cups; pages 30–31), drained

1 seedless medium cucumber, cut into ¼-inch pieces

4½ ounces crumbled feta cheese (1 cup)

⅓ cup chopped fresh cilantro, plus more for garnish

3 scallions, thinly sliced

¼ cup extra-virgin olive oil

3 tablespoons fresh lime juice, plus wedges for serving

Coarse salt and freshly ground pepper

Place beans, cucumber, feta, cilantro, scallions, oil, and lime juice in a large bowl. Season with 1 teaspoon salt and ½ teaspoon pepper, and toss well to combine. Top with cilantro and serve with lime wedges.

CRISP BLACK-BEAN QUESADILLAS

These uncomplicated quesadillas make a rewarding meatless lunch, snack, or dinner (add a big green salad with toasted pepitas and a side of guacamole). Serve with sour cream or crema, salsa, lime wedges, and sliced pickled jalapeños. Silky and smooth when mashed, the black beans contrast nicely with the crisp corn tortillas.

MAKES 12 QUESADILLAS

2 cups cooked black beans (pages 30–31), drained

1 cup coarsely grated Monterey Jack cheese (4 ounces)

½ cup finely chopped white onion

¼ cup finely chopped pickled jalapeño chiles, plus more, sliced, for serving

2 tablespoons chopped fresh cilantro

1 teaspoon ground cumin

Coarse salt

12 (7-inch) corn tortillas

¼ cup plus 2 tablespoons vegetable oil

Sour cream, salsa, sliced pickled jalapeños, and lime wedges, for serving

1. In a medium bowl, mash beans until smooth, using a potato masher or back of a large spoon. Add cheese, onion, pickled jalapenos, cilantro, cumin, and ¾ teaspoon salt, and stir to combine. Place about ¼ cup bean mixture on one side of each corn tortilla, then fold tortilla in half, pressing on bean mixture to flatten.

2. Heat 2 tablespoons oil in a large skillet over medium until shimmering, about 2 minutes. Working in batches, add 4 quesadillas to skillet and cook, turning once, until browned in places, about 4 minutes total. Transfer to a serving platter. Repeat with remaining oil and quesadillas. Serve with sour cream, salsa, sliced jalapeños, and lime wedges.

SPAGHETTI WITH WHITE BEANS AND ANCHOVIES

Anchovy paste, made from ground anchovies, salt, and oil, is the secret weapon in this flavorful pasta dish. Used in small doses, the paste brings a savory punch to all kinds of recipes without revealing itself as an ingredient. As important as the anchovy paste here are the breadcrumbs—don't skimp on them, since they add a welcome crunch.

SERVES 6 TO 8

Coarse salt and freshly ground pepper

¼ cup extra-virgin olive oil

1 cup fresh breadcrumbs

3 garlic cloves, thinly sliced

½ teaspoon red-pepper flakes

2 tablespoons anchovy paste

3 cups cooked white beans (pages 30–31), drained

2 tablespoons capers in brine, drained and chopped

1 pound pasta, such as spaghetti

½ cup finely chopped fresh flat-leaf parsley

Finely grated Parmigiano-Reggiano cheese, for serving

1. Bring a large pot of salted water to a boil. Heat oil in a large skillet over medium-high. Add breadcrumbs and cook, stirring occasionally, until golden, about 6 minutes. Add garlic, red-pepper flakes, and anchovy paste, and cook, stirring, until garlic is golden, about 2 minutes. Add white beans and capers, stirring to combine.

2. Cook pasta until al dente according to package instructions. Drain pasta, reserving 1 cup cooking water. Toss pasta with bean mixture, adding some reserved cooking water. Add parsley and toss to combine; season with salt and pepper. Serve topped with grated cheese.

PRESERVED-LEMON AND WHITE-BEAN SPREAD

Pressure-cooked beans tend to be creamier and purée more smoothly than their canned counterparts, making them perfect for dips and spreads. This vegan-friendly spread is punctuated with mellow "pressure-roasted" garlic, chopped fresh herbs, smoked paprika, and preserved lemon, the not-so-secret ingredient that brightens many Moroccan and Middle Eastern specialties. Look for jarred preserved lemons at specialty grocers.

MAKES ABOUT 3 CUPS

3 cups cooked white beans (pages 30–31), drained

1 head "pressure-roasted" garlic (recipe at right), cloves peeled

3 tablespoons extra-virgin olive oil

2 tablespoons finely chopped preserved lemon (peel and flesh)

1½ tablespoons fresh lemon juice, or to taste

½ teaspoon smoked paprika

2 tablespoons finely chopped fresh dill

2 tablespoons finely chopped fresh mint

¾ teaspoon coarse salt

1 baguette, thinly sliced and toasted, for serving

In a food processor, pulse beans, garlic, oil, preserved lemon, lemon juice, paprika, dill, mint, and salt until smooth. Serve with toasted baguette slices.

"Pressure-roasted" **GARLIC** has the same sweet, nutty, mellow character of traditionally caramelized garlic heads. Cut top ¼ inch off 4 heads of garlic to expose cloves, then sprinkle with coarse salt. Wrap separately in parchment-lined foil. Pour 2½ cups water into pressure cooker, and stack garlic on rack. If using stovetop cooker, secure lid and bring to pressure over medium-high heat; reduce heat to maintain pressure and cook for 15 minutes. Remove from heat, quickly release pressure, then remove lid. If using electric, secure lid and manually set cooker to 20 minutes. Once time is complete, turn off, quickly release pressure, then remove lid. Let garlic cool, then peel cloves.

PASTA E FAGIOLI WITH ESCAROLE

Every cook makes this classic Italian soup his or her own. This version is almost stewlike, beginning with a tomato sauce that's reduced until it is concentrated and thick. Instead of water or chicken broth as the liquid base, this recipe features the cooking liquid for the pressure-cooked beans, creating a richer stock.

──────────────── **SERVES 6 TO 8** ────────────────

3 tablespoons extra-virgin olive oil

1 medium onion, finely chopped

2 garlic cloves, smashed

3 medium carrots, finely chopped

1 can (28 ounces) whole tomatoes

1 Parmigiano-Reggiano cheese rind, plus shaved cheese for serving (optional)

2 tablespoons capers in brine, drained and chopped

1 rosemary sprig

1 dried bay leaf

Pinch red-pepper flakes

Cooked white beans (about 6 cups; pages 30–31), cooking liquid reserved

1 cup ditalini pasta

½ pound escarole, coarsely chopped

Coarse salt

1. Heat oil in a large pot over medium-high. Add onion, garlic, and carrots, and cook, stirring occasionally, until golden, about 6 minutes. Add tomatoes (with their juices), stirring and breaking up tomatoes with a wooden spoon. Add parmesan rind, capers, rosemary, bay leaf, and red-pepper flakes, and cook until reduced to a thick sauce, 10 to 15 minutes. Add white beans and reserved cooking liquid, stirring to combine.

2. Add pasta and bring to a boil. Cook pasta until al dente, about 8 minutes. Stir in escarole and cook until wilted, about 1 minute. (Discard cheese rind, rosemary sprig, and bay leaf.) Season with salt and serve with cheese, if desired.

Have a pot of pasta e fagioli **READY IN ADVANCE.** Cook the soup through Step 1, then cool completely and refrigerate. When you're ready to serve it, bring the soup to a boil and add the pasta and escarole.

MOLASSES-BAKED BEANS WITH BACON

Sweet, dark, syrupy molasses combines with sharp Dijon mustard and pleasantly salty ham stock to give giant white beans, or gigantes, a wonderful flavor. Although the beans are fully cooked to begin with, they bake for an additional 90 minutes or so in the casserole without falling apart. (You can substitute other beans, including Great Northern, for the gigantes, if you like.) Topped with tender slices of onion and strips of bacon, this is a robust side dish; adding the optional ham (used for the stock) makes it a one-pot supper.

SERVES 8

Unsalted butter, for dish

1 cup Ham Stock (page 25)

1 can (14.5 ounces) crushed tomatoes

¼ cup unsulfured molasses

2 tablespoons Dijon mustard

Coarse salt and freshly ground pepper

Cooked gigante beans (about 6 cups; pages 30–31), drained

2 cups cooked diced ham (optional; page 25)

1 large Vidalia onion, sliced into ¼-inch-thick rounds

½ pound thick-cut bacon

1. Preheat oven to 400°F. Butter a 3-quart shallow baking dish.

2. In a large bowl, whisk ham stock, tomatoes, molasses, and mustard until smooth. Season with ½ teaspoon salt and ¼ teaspoon pepper. Add gigante beans and ham, if desired.

3. Transfer bean mixture to prepared baking dish. Top with sliced onion, pressing into liquid. Top with a layer of bacon. Transfer dish to a rimmed baking sheet, and bake until beans have absorbed most of liquid and bacon is browned, about 90 minutes.

LENTIL AND ARUGULA SALAD

When using lentils (or any other legume), it's important to dress them while they are still warm, then let them stand for about ten minutes to allow the flavors to meld. We also cooked the lentils with the aromatics for an extra hit of seasoning. We've chosen green (sometimes labeled "French") lentils for the pressure cooker because they stay firm even after cooking, unlike the more common (and delicate) brown variety, which can get too soft in the machine.

SERVES 8

6 cups water

2 cups French green lentils, picked over and rinsed

1 garlic clove, minced

1 tablespoon thinly sliced peeled fresh ginger

1 teaspoon smoked paprika

1 teaspoon curry powder

Coarse salt

2 medium carrots, thinly sliced

1 jalapeño, finely chopped

2 tablespoons extra-virgin olive oil

2 tablespoons rice vinegar

½ cup chopped fresh cilantro

6 ounces arugula

1. Combine the water, lentils, garlic, ginger, paprika, curry powder, and 2 teaspoons salt in a 6- to 8-quart pressure cooker.

2. **STOVETOP:** Secure lid. Bring to high pressure over medium-high heat; reduce heat to maintain pressure and cook for 6 minutes. Remove from heat, quickly release pressure, then remove lid.

   ELECTRIC: Secure lid. Manually set cooker to 8 minutes and let it come to pressure. Once time is complete, turn off, quickly release pressure, then remove lid.

3. Stir in carrots, jalapeño, oil, vinegar, and cilantro. Season with salt and let stand 10 minutes. Toss with arugula and serve.

GREEK LENTIL SOUP

Rustic, homey *fakes soupa,* or lentil soup, is Greek comfort food at its very best. It is typically finished at the table with a splash of red-wine vinegar (we prefer the brightness of lemon juice here) and olive oil, with guests adjusting the amounts to suit their own tastes. Two heads of garlic may seem excessive, but the pressure cooker mellows their bite, rendering them more sweet than sharp. Serve the soup with fresh feta, toasted pita, and olives.

SERVES 6

2 quarts water

2 cups French green lentils, picked over and rinsed

2 garlic heads, cloves separated and peeled

2 medium onions, finely chopped

1 large carrot, finely chopped

1 large celery stalk, finely chopped

2 tablespoons chopped fresh thyme

¼ cup extra-virgin olive oil, plus more for serving

Coarse salt and freshly ground pepper

2 tablespoons fresh lemon juice, plus wedges for serving

¼ cup chopped fresh flat-leaf parsley or dill

1. Place the water, lentils, garlic, onions, carrot, celery, thyme, 2 tablespoons oil, and 2 teaspoons salt in a 6- to 8-quart pressure cooker.

2. **STOVETOP:** Secure lid. Bring to high pressure over medium-high heat; reduce heat to maintain pressure and cook for 12 minutes. Remove from heat, quickly release pressure, then remove lid.

   ELECTRIC: Secure lid. Manually set cooker to 15 minutes and let it come to pressure. Once time is complete, turn off, quickly release pressure, then remove lid.

3. Add lemon juice, 1 teaspoon pepper, and remaining 2 tablespoons oil. Mash garlic cloves with the back of a fork; stir in garlic and parsley. Serve with lemon wedges and olive oil.

FRENCH LENTILS WITH MUSTARD-TARRAGON BUTTER

Lentils are a classic accompaniment to salmon, particularly in France, but also work beautifully with roast chicken or sausages. Here, they are paired with a compound butter made with the unbeatable combination of mustard (both Dijon and grainy), tarragon, and parsley.

SERVES 8

- 2 tablespoons extra-virgin olive oil
- 1 medium onion, finely chopped
- 1 large carrot, finely chopped
- 1 large celery stalk, finely chopped
- 4 tablespoons unsalted butter, softened
- ¼ cup chopped fresh flat-leaf parsley
- 1 teaspoon Dijon mustard
- 1 teaspoon grainy mustard
- 1 teaspoon finely chopped fresh tarragon, plus sprigs for garnish
- 1 teaspoon fresh lemon juice
- Coarse salt and freshly ground pepper
- 5 cups cooked French green lentils (pages 30–31), drained

1. Heat oil in a large skillet over medium-high. Add onion, carrot, and celery, and cook, stirring occasionally, until softened, 3 to 5 minutes.

2. Meanwhile, stir together butter, parsley, both mustards, tarragon, lemon juice, and ½ teaspoon each salt and pepper.

3. Combine lentils and vegetable mixture in a large bowl. Add butter mixture and stir until melted. Season with salt and pepper. Top with tarragon sprigs and serve.

BROWN RICE

PEARL BARLEY

FARRO

JASMINE RICE

FREEKEH

STEEL-CUT OATS

PRESSURE-COOKED GRAINS

Cooking a pot of rice, farro, barley, or other grains in the pressure cooker takes about a third of the time it would by traditional stovetop methods. During testing, we found times ranged based on the model of cooker and the age of the grains. Use the chart at right for guidance on cooking times that result in grains that are tender and intact (they should still have a little bite). We also found that, with the exception of rice and oats, toasting before cooking enhances the flavor of grains. For white and brown rice, we recommend a short cooking time under high pressure with a natural release to allow it to steam further.

As with beans, there is a potential for foaming when cooking grains, but adding a tablespoon of oil to the cooking water should help. As a further precaution, cover the vent with a clean kitchen towel when you vent the steam. This will help absorb some of that foam and avoid a messier release.

1 cup grain of choice (see chart at right)

Water (see chart at right)

1 tablespoon extra-virgin olive oil (or unsalted butter; use butter for oatmeal)

½ teaspoon coarse salt

1. Toast grain (except rice or steel-cut oats):

   STOVETOP: Heat a 6- to 8-quart pressure cooker over medium-low. Add grain and toast, stirring, until fragrant, about 5 minutes.

   ELECTRIC: Set a 6- to 8-quart pressure cooker to sauté. Add grain and toast, stirring, until fragrant, about 3 minutes.

2. Add water, rice or steel-cut oats (if using), oil, and salt to pressure cooker.

   STOVETOP: Secure lid. Bring to high pressure over medium-high heat; reduce heat to maintain pressure and cook according to time provided for each type of grain. Remove from heat, quickly release pressure (loosely cover vent with a clean kitchen towel), then remove lid. (For rice, let pressure decrease naturally.) Drain, if necessary.

   ELECTRIC: Secure lid. Manually set cooker to time provided for each type of grain and let it come to pressure. Once time is complete, turn off, quickly release pressure (loosely cover vent with a clean kitchen towel), then remove lid. (For rice, let pressure decrease naturally.) Drain, if necessary.

GRAIN (1 CUP)	WATER	STOVETOP PRESSURE COOKER	ELECTRIC PRESSURE COOKER	YIELD
JASMINE RICE, RINSED AND DRAINED	1¼ CUPS FOR STOVETOP; 1 CUP FOR ELECTRIC	3-5 MINUTES + 10 MINUTES NATURAL RELEASE	3-5 MINUTES + 10 MINUTES NATURAL RELEASE	3 CUPS
BROWN RICE	3 CUPS FOR STOVETOP; 1½ CUPS FOR ELECTRIC	12-15 MINUTES + 10 MINUTES NATURAL RELEASE	15-20 MINUTES + 10 MINUTES NATURAL RELEASE	3 CUPS
WILD RICE	4 CUPS	15-20 MINUTES	15-20 MINUTES	2¼ CUPS
STEEL-CUT OATS	3½ CUPS	10-15 MINUTES	15-20 MINUTES	3 CUPS
FARRO	4 CUPS	15-22 MINUTES	18-22 MINUTES	2½ CUPS
FREEKEH	4 CUPS	3-8 MINUTES	5-10 MINUTES	3 CUPS
PEARL BARLEY	4 CUPS	12-17 MINUTES	12-17 MINUTES	3 CUPS

FRIED BROWN RICE WITH SHRIMP

Fried rice is an excellent way to use up cooked rice—or a good excuse to cook a fresh pot (especially when it's this fast!). Starting with brown rice (instead of white) means you don't have to chill it before frying. The frying process is made easy with the addition of smoked Chinese sausage, which contributes a generous amount of fat to the mix and blends nicely with the mellow shrimp. (Use Spanish chorizo if you can't find Chinese sausage.)

SERVES 6 TO 8

3 tablespoons vegetable oil

8 ounces Chinese sausage or Spanish chorizo, thinly sliced

2 shallots, thinly sliced

2 tablespoons finely chopped peeled fresh ginger

3 garlic cloves, thinly sliced

6 cups cooked long-grain brown rice (pages 66–67), drained

Coarse salt

1 pound medium shrimp (26 to 30 count), peeled, deveined, and halved crosswise

2 tablespoons toasted sesame oil

Chopped fresh cilantro, for garnish

Chili sauce, for serving

Heat oil in a large skillet over medium. Add sausage, shallots, ginger, and garlic, and cook, stirring, until fragrant, about 2 minutes. Add rice and 1 teaspoon salt, and cook, stirring occasionally and pressing down with a wooden spoon, until rice is crisp, about 8 minutes. Add shrimp and cook, stirring frequently, until just cooked through, about 2 minutes. Drizzle with sesame oil, top with cilantro, and serve with chili sauce.

FREEKEH, CAULIFLOWER, AND HERB SALAD

Freekeh is an ancient grain that has become widely popular owing to its nutritious and delicious qualities. Young green wheat is picked at its peak and then roasted and cracked. (You can also buy whole freekeh, which takes about 20 minutes longer to cook.) If you prepare a large batch of freekeh in the pressure cooker, you can refrigerate it for up to five days, using a bit at a time. We like to serve it for lunch with flatbread and labneh, but it's also fantastic as a side dish.

SERVES 6 TO 8

---

2 cups cooked cracked freekeh (pages 66–67), drained

1 small head cooked cauliflower (pages 86–87)

2 tablespoons extra-virgin olive oil

2 garlic cloves, minced

½ teaspoon curry powder

½ teaspoon ground cumin

3 strips lemon zest, plus 1 to 2 tablespoons fresh lemon juice, to taste

½ cup chopped fresh flat-leaf parsley

¼ cup chopped fresh dill

Coarse salt and freshly ground pepper

Grilled flatbread and labneh, for serving (optional)

Toss to combine freekeh and cauliflower in a large bowl. Heat oil in a small skillet over medium-low. Add garlic and cook until fragrant, about 2 minutes. Add curry powder and cumin, and cook, stirring, 1 minute. Add lemon zest and juice. Pour mixture over freekeh and cauliflower. Toss with parsley, dill, ½ teaspoon pepper, and salt to taste, before serving with grilled flatbread and labneh (if desired).

FARRO WITH CORN, SHISHITOS, AND CHERRY TOMATOES

Chewy, nutty farro makes a robust base for grain bowls, risottos, and main-course salads such as this one. It's also an underappreciated match for high-summer produce—think ripe tomatoes, corn, fragrant basil, and peppers (we like shishitos). For this recipe, sauté the vegetables while the farro cooks, to ensure the grain is served warm.

SERVES 4

4 tablespoons unsalted butter

1 pint shishito peppers
or 2 green bell peppers,
seeded and thinly sliced

½ cup thinly sliced scallions
(white and light-green
parts only)

2 large garlic cloves, minced

3 cups fresh corn kernels
(from 4 to 5 ears of corn)

Coarse salt and freshly
ground pepper

1 pint cherry tomatoes

4 cups cooked farro
(pages 66–67), kept warm

Basil sprigs, for garnish

Melt butter in a large skillet over medium-low heat. Add peppers, scallions, and garlic, and cook, stirring, until peppers are blistered, 3 to 5 minutes. Add corn, 1 teaspoon salt, and ½ teaspoon pepper, and cook, stirring, 2 minutes. Add cherry tomatoes and cook, stirring, just until tomatoes are heated through, about 2 minutes. Transfer vegetables to a platter with warm farro, top with basil, and serve.

SHISHITO, a Japanese chile, is generally mild; however, one out of every ten is delightfully spicy. You can find them at farmers' markets in summer, and increasingly at specialty grocers.

STEEL-CUT OATMEAL

Coarsely chopped steel-cut oats are far tastier than rolled oats, but they usually require an overnight soak before they can be cooked on the stovetop. In the pressure cooker, however, you can have a bowl of steel-cut oats for breakfast in 20 minutes, no presoaking required. Top each serving with fresh fruit, nuts, whole-milk yogurt, maple syrup, honey, or even something savory like avocado or a poached egg. Once cooked, the oatmeal can be refrigerated for up to five days; individual portions can be warmed with a little milk on the stovetop over low heat.

SERVES 6 TO 8

7 cups water

2 cups steel-cut oats

1 tablespoon unsalted butter, plus more for serving

Coarse salt

½ cup milk, plus more for serving

1. Combine the water, oats, butter, and ½ teaspoon salt in a 6- to 8-quart pressure cooker.

2. **STOVETOP:** Secure lid. Bring to high pressure over medium-high heat; reduce heat to maintain pressure and cook for 12 minutes. Remove from heat, quickly release pressure (loosely cover vent with a clean kitchen towel), then remove lid.

   ELECTRIC: Secure lid. Manually set cooker to 20 minutes and let it come to pressure. Once time is complete, turn off, quickly release pressure (loosely cover vent with a clean kitchen towel), then remove lid.

3. Stir in milk; serve with additional milk and butter, and top as desired.

Mix up your **TOPPING** choices with any of the following:

- Sliced bananas, brown sugar, and a touch of cream

- Fresh berries and honey

- Chopped dried fruit, such as prunes, figs, or apricots; sliced almonds; and maple syrup

- Sliced fresh figs, toasted walnuts, and honey

- Coarsely chopped pistachios and chai sugar (½ cup granulated sugar mixed with 2 teaspoons cinnamon, 2 teaspoons ground cardamom, and 1 teaspoon freshly grated nutmeg)

CREAMY POLENTA

Beginning with the same basic recipe for polenta, you can invent a wide variety of dishes. First, we made it even creamier by adding crème fraîche and topped it with roasted tomatoes and herbs (page 79); next we spiced it up with cayenne and shrimp (page 80), and finally, we served it firm for breakfast (chilling it does the trick), after dusting it with cheese and letting it crisp under the broiler (page 83).

If the thought of all that stirring keeps you from making polenta more often, the pressure cooker may change your mind. The machine's intense bubbling creates continuous movement, preventing lumps without constant stirring. Nevertheless, if your pressure-cooker polenta seems a little thin, whisk it for a few additional minutes over medium-high heat (stovetop models) or while using the sauté function (electric models). Then serve it with absolutely everything—like pork shoulder (page 125), sautéed peaches, and peppery arugula, as shown here.

MAKES ABOUT 5 CUPS

4 cups water

1⅓ cups coarsely ground yellow cornmeal

1¼ teaspoons coarse salt

2 tablespoons unsalted butter

½ cup finely grated Parmigiano-Reggiano cheese (2 ounces)

1. In a 6- to 8-quart pressure cooker, whisk together the water, cornmeal, and salt.

2. **STOVETOP:** Secure lid. Bring to high pressure over medium-high heat; reduce heat to maintain pressure and cook for 6 minutes. Remove from heat and let pressure decrease naturally for 6 minutes. Release remaining pressure, if necessary, then remove lid.

   ELECTRIC: Secure lid. Manually set cooker to 14 minutes and let it come to pressure. Once time is complete, turn off, quickly release pressure, then remove lid.

3. Add butter and cheese, and stir until butter is incorporated and mixture has thickened slightly, about 2 minutes.

POLENTA WITH ROASTED CHERRY TOMATOES AND CRÈME FRAÎCHE

Smooth polenta is the perfect canvas for all kinds of savory (and even some sweet) finishes. Here, crème fraîche gets whisked into the pressure-cooked Creamy Polenta to create a velvety texture. It's topped with roasted sweet-tart cherry tomatoes, another dollop of crème fraîche, fresh herbs, and parmesan shavings. Serve as a main course, or as a standout side dish with roasted chicken or pork.

SERVES 6

2 pints cherry tomatoes, halved

¼ cup extra-virgin olive oil

4 garlic cloves, smashed

6 mixed herb sprigs, such as rosemary, oregano, marjoram, thyme, and mint, plus more for garnish

1 teaspoon coarse salt

½ teaspoon freshly ground pepper

Creamy Polenta (page 76)

8 ounces crème fraîche

Shaved Parmigiano-Reggiano cheese, for serving

1. Preheat oven to 400°F. Toss tomatoes, oil, garlic, herbs, salt, and pepper on a rimmed baking sheet. Roast tomatoes until bursting, 20 to 25 minutes, tossing occasionally.

2. Meanwhile, make the polenta. Whisk half the crème fraîche into polenta; transfer polenta to serving bowls. Serve topped with roasted tomatoes, remaining crème fraîche, herbs, and cheese shavings.

SPICY SHRIMP AND POLENTA

In a twist on one of the tastiest simple dishes to come out of the South—Low Country shrimp and grits—polenta takes center stage. The yellow corn variety used for polenta is different from the white one used for grits, but both are coarsely stone-ground, and the creamy nature of the dish remains, made creamier still with cheese. Here, we replaced the parmesan and butter with a sharp cheddar, stirred in after pressure-cooking the cornmeal.

SERVES 4 TO 6

Creamy Polenta (page 76; omit butter and Parmigiano-Reggiano cheese)

1 cup grated sharp cheddar cheese (4 ounces)

4 strips bacon, cut crosswise into ¼-inch pieces

1 tablespoon unsalted butter

½ cup finely chopped green bell pepper

1 garlic clove, finely chopped

1 pound medium shrimp (26 to 30 count), peeled and deveined, with tails intact if desired

½ teaspoon cayenne pepper

Coarse salt and freshly ground black pepper

3 scallions (white and pale-green parts only), thinly sliced

1. Make the polenta; stir in cheddar and cover to keep warm.

2. Meanwhile, cook bacon in a large skillet over medium heat until crisp, about 8 minutes. Using a slotted spoon, transfer bacon to a paper-towel–lined plate; reserve fat in skillet.

3. Melt butter in skillet over medium heat. Add bell pepper and garlic, and cook, stirring, until softened, about 5 minutes. In a medium bowl, toss shrimp with cayenne, 1 teaspoon salt, and ½ teaspoon black pepper. Add shrimp to skillet and cook until just opaque throughout, about 3 minutes. Add scallions and toss occasionally, until wilted, about 1 minute. Serve polenta topped with shrimp and reserved bacon.

POLENTA SQUARES WITH ASPARAGUS AND POACHED EGGS

In a versatile dish that works for breakfast, lunch, or dinner, eggs and asparagus meet and get along beautifully, with polenta squares as their base. Simply start by making Creamy Polenta, then spread it on a rimmed baking sheet and chill until firm—at least 1 hour or up to 1 day—before broiling with cheese. The tender yolk from a poached egg creates a silky sauce.

SERVES 6 TO 12

Creamy Polenta (page 76)

2 tablespoons extra-virgin olive oil, plus more for pan

1 cup finely grated Parmigiano-Reggiano cheese (4 ounces), plus more for serving

1 bunch thin asparagus (about 1 pound), trimmed

Coarse salt and freshly ground pepper

12 large eggs

1. Spread polenta evenly in an oiled 9-by-13-inch rimmed baking sheet or baking pan. Chill until firm, at least 1 hour or up to overnight.

2. Preheat broiler with rack 4 inches from the heat source. Fill a large, deep skillet with water three-quarters full and bring to a gentle simmer.

3. Cut polenta into 12 squares and sprinkle generously with cheese. Broil until cheese is golden, about 5 minutes.

4. Toss asparagus with oil on a second rimmed baking sheet. Season with salt and pepper. Spread in a single layer and broil, tossing occasionally, until tender and browned in spots, about 5 minutes.

5. Crack eggs, one at a time, into barely simmering water. Cook until whites are just set and yolks are still runny, about 3 minutes.

6. Meanwhile, transfer polenta squares to plates. Using a slotted spoon, remove each egg from water; blot bottom of spoon on a paper towel, then transfer egg to sit atop polenta square. Season with salt and pepper, and sprinkle with cheese. Serve with asparagus.

WINTER SQUASH

POTATOES

BROCCOLI

CAULIFLOWER

CARROTS

BEETS

PRESSURE-COOKED VEGETABLES

The pressure cooker allows for surprising versatility in preparing vegetables, playing up their individual flavor profiles. Steam them in mere minutes for use in a luxurious soup, a creamy mash, or a satisfying salad.

Using a 1-inch-high rack and a steamer insert will create a true steam, but you can also just put everything directly in the pressure cooker. For individual cooking times, see the chart at right. The shorter times given are for just-tender vegetables to enjoy as is or in a salad or side dish, while longer times yield vegetables that are tender enough for mashing or blending into soup.

MAKES 1 TO 3 POUNDS

3 cups water

1 teaspoon coarse salt

1 to 3 pounds vegetables, peeled if necessary (see chart at right)

1. Place rack, if using, in a 6- to 8-quart pressure cooker. Add the water and salt. Place vegetables in steamer insert, if using, or directly in pressure cooker.

2. **STOVETOP:** Secure lid. Bring to high pressure over medium-high heat; reduce heat to maintain pressure and cook according to time provided for each type of vegetable. Remove from heat, quickly release pressure, then remove lid.

   ELECTRIC: Secure lid. Manually set cooker to time provided for each type of vegetable and let it come to pressure. Once time is complete, turn off, quickly release pressure, then remove lid.

3. Drain vegetables, if necessary.

VEGETABLE	SIZE	STOVETOP	ELECTRIC
POTATOES	1-INCH PIECES	1-2 MINUTES	1-3 MINUTES
BEETS*	1-INCH PIECES	3-10 MINUTES	4-8 MINUTES
CAULIFLOWER	2-INCH FLORETS	0-1 MINUTE	0-1 MINUTE
BROCCOLI	2-INCH FLORETS	0 MINUTES	0 MINUTES
WINTER SQUASH (BUTTERNUT, ACORN, KABOCHA)	1-INCH PIECES	1-3 MINUTES	1-3 MINUTES
CARROTS	1-INCH PIECES	3-4 MINUTES	3-4 MINUTES

*For whole beets, cook 25 minutes in a stovetop or electric pressure cooker.

When a recipe calls for **0 MINUTES,** set the timer to 1, but turn off the cooker as soon as it comes to pressure.

CARROT SOUP WITH CUMIN
AND GINGER

BROCCOLI AND
PARMESAN SOUP

BEET SOUP WITH
SOUR CREAM AND DILL

POTATO SOUP WITH
ALL THE TOPPINGS

CAULIFLOWER SOUP WITH
CARAWAY SEEDS

BUTTERNUT SQUASH SOUP WITH
PISTACHIO OIL

POTATO SOUP WITH ALL THE TOPPINGS

A hearty bowl of "loaded baked potato soup"—served with an array of savory toppings—is downright addictive, and beginning with pressure-cooked russet potatoes produces an ultra-smooth texture. The accompaniments here are merely suggestions; you can get as creative as you choose. The possibilities are (nearly) limitless.

SERVES 6

6 slices bacon, chopped

1 medium onion, chopped

3 garlic cloves, minced

Coarse salt and freshly ground pepper

¼ cup all-purpose flour

1 medium carrot, chopped

1 large celery stalk, chopped

6 cups Chicken or Vegetable Stock, homemade (pages 24 or 26) or store-bought

2 cups whole milk

2 pounds cooked potatoes, preferably russet (pages 86–87), drained

Grated cheddar cheese, sour cream, sliced scallions or snipped chives, for serving

1. In a large pot over medium heat, cook bacon until crisp, about 8 minutes. Using a slotted spoon, transfer bacon to a paper-towel–lined plate; reserve fat in pot. Add onion, garlic, 1 teaspoon salt, and ¼ teaspoon pepper, and cook, stirring occasionally, until golden and softened, about 6 minutes. Stir in flour and cook, stirring, 1 minute. Add carrot, celery, stock, and milk; bring to a boil and cook until carrot is tender, about 8 minutes. Add potatoes. Let cool slightly. Skim any fat from surface.

2. Working in batches, purée mixture in a blender or with an immersion blender until smooth. Return to pot and reheat over medium; season with salt and pepper. Serve topped with reserved bacon and accompaniments, as desired.

CARROT SOUP WITH CUMIN AND GINGER

Fresh ginger and warm spices create an incredibly aromatic, creamy carrot soup. Adding the ginger raw to the blender, instead of cooking it first, allows it to retain more of its pronounced spicy character, while the sweetness of a diced apple helps keep things balanced. For a richer soup, substitute heavy cream for the half-and-half.

SERVES 6 TO 8

4 tablespoons unsalted butter

1 medium onion, coarsely chopped

Coarse salt and freshly ground pepper

2 quarts water

1 apple, peeled, cored, and chopped

1 dried bay leaf

1 teaspoon coriander seeds

½ teaspoon cumin seeds

3 pounds cooked carrots (pages 86–87), drained

½ cup half-and-half

2 tablespoons minced peeled fresh ginger

1. Melt butter in a large pot over medium-high heat. Add onion, 1 teaspoon salt, and ½ teaspoon pepper. Cook, stirring occasionally, until onion is golden, about 6 minutes. Add the water, apple, bay leaf, coriander seeds, and cumin seeds, and cook, stirring, until apple is tender, about 10 minutes. Add carrots, half-and-half, and ginger. Let cool slightly. (Discard bay leaf.)

2. Working in batches, purée mixture in a blender or with an immersion blender until smooth. Season with salt and pepper. Serve immediately.

BROCCOLI AND PARMESAN SOUP

Parmesan cheese offers a richer, more complex nuttiness than cream alone, making this soup an excellent upgrade from the classic childhood pairing of broccoli and cheese. Be sure to boil down the wine in this soup before adding the stock—this helps concentrate the flavors and minimizes the alcohol content more efficiently than when added with another liquid.

SERVES 4 TO 6

- 2 tablespoons unsalted butter
- 1 medium onion, finely chopped
- ½ cup dry white wine
- 2½ cups Chicken Stock, homemade (page 24) or store-bought
- 1¼ pounds cooked broccoli (pages 86–87), drained

  Coarse salt and freshly ground pepper
- ½ cup heavy cream
- ½ cup finely grated Parmigiano-Reggiano cheese (about 2 ounces), plus shavings for serving

  Extra-virgin olive oil, for drizzling (optional)

1. Melt butter in a large pot over medium-low heat. Add onion and cook, stirring, until softened, about 5 minutes. Add wine and bring to a boil; cook until most of liquid has evaporated. Add stock, broccoli, 1 teaspoon salt, and ½ teaspoon pepper, and bring to a boil. Remove from heat and let cool slightly.

2. Working in batches, purée mixture in a blender or with an immersion blender until almost smooth. Add cream and grated cheese, and bring just to a simmer over medium-high heat (do not let boil). Season with salt and pepper. Drizzle with oil, top with cheese shavings, and serve immediately.

BEET SOUP WITH SOUR CREAM AND DILL

This soup makes good use of the beets' cooking liquid—it lends sweetness (but not too much) and a gorgeous color. Harissa adds a little heat, and vinegar contributes just the right amount of acid.

SERVES 6 TO 8

2 tablespoons extra-virgin olive oil

2 medium red onions, coarsely chopped

2 garlic cloves, smashed

1 tablespoon harissa

3 pounds cooked beets, (pages 86–87), plus cooking liquid

1 quart Chicken, Vegetable, or Ham Stock, homemade (pages 24–26) or store-bought

1 to 2 tablespoons apple cider vinegar, to taste

Coarse salt and freshly ground pepper

Sour cream, for serving

Coarsely chopped fresh dill, for garnish

1. Heat oil in a large pot over medium-high. Add onions and garlic and cook, stirring occasionally, until golden and softened, about 6 minutes. Add harissa and cook until a few shades darker, about 1 minute. Add beets and reserved cooking liquid, stock, 1 tablespoon vinegar, 1 teaspoon salt, and ½ teaspoon pepper, and stir to combine. Bring to a simmer, then remove from heat. Let cool slightly.

2. Working in batches, purée mixture in a blender or with an immersion blender until smooth. Season with salt and pepper. Top with sour cream and dill, and serve.

If you don't have **HARISSA** on hand, substitute a mixture of tomato paste and smoked paprika, to your taste.

CAULIFLOWER SOUP WITH CARAWAY SEEDS

Caraway seeds are most commonly associated with rye bread and sauerkraut. But the seeds are a welcome addition to many soups, salads, and cooked vegetables, including turnips, beets, and cauliflower. This pressure-cooked cauliflower is seasoned with just enough caraway seed, while yogurt adds a little acidity. It's important to use whole-milk yogurt and to keep the soup from coming to a boil once the yogurt is added (otherwise it will break).

—————————— **SERVES 6 TO 8** ——————————

- 3 tablespoons unsalted butter
- 1 medium onion, chopped
- 1 teaspoon caraway seeds, plus more, toasted, for garnish
- 2½ cups Chicken Stock, homemade (page 24) or store-bought, or water
- 2 pounds cooked cauliflower (pages 86–87), drained

  Coarse salt and freshly ground pepper
- ¾ cup plain whole-milk yogurt, plus more for serving

  Finely chopped fresh cilantro, for garnish

1. Melt butter in a large pot over medium-low heat. Add onion and caraway seeds and cook, stirring, until softened, about 6 minutes. Add stock, cauliflower, 1 teaspoon salt, and ½ teaspoon pepper, and bring to a boil. Remove from heat and let cool slightly.

2. Working in batches, purée mixture in a blender or with an immersion blender until smooth. Bring to a simmer and stir in yogurt just until heated through (do not let boil). Season with salt and pepper. Top with yogurt, cilantro, and caraway seeds, and serve.

BUTTERNUT SQUASH SOUP WITH PISTACHIO OIL

A drizzle of nut oil, common in French cooking, can elevate a wide range of foods—delicate salad greens, a sautéed fish fillet, or a puréed vegetable soup, for example. These finishing oils can be expensive and difficult to find in the States, however, and they don't keep well. But with a food processor, you can make your own nut oils quickly and easily: Simply blend pistachios with extra-virgin olive oil to drizzle over winter squash soup. The pistachios will not be completely ground, but you can save a few pieces when you strain the oil to use as a garnish.

SERVES 4 TO 6

- 4 tablespoons unsalted butter
- 1 medium onion, coarsely chopped
- ½ cup dry white wine
- 3 cups Chicken Stock, homemade (page 24) or store-bought
- 2 pounds cooked butternut squash (pages 86–87), drained

  Coarse salt and freshly ground pepper
- ¼ cup shelled unsalted pistachios
- ¼ cup extra-virgin olive oil

1. Melt 2 tablespoons butter in a large pot over medium-low heat. Add onion and cook, stirring, until softened, about 6 minutes. Add wine, bring to a boil, and cook until most of liquid has evaporated. Add stock, butternut squash, 1 teaspoon salt, and ½ teaspoon pepper. Bring to a simmer, then remove from heat. Let cool slightly.

2. Meanwhile, pulse pistachios and oil in a food processor until smooth with a few pieces remaining, 1 minute. Pour mixture through a fine-mesh sieve set over a large bowl (do not press on solids, but reserve larger pieces).

3. Working in batches, purée butternut squash mixture in a blender or with an immersion blender until smooth. Return pot to heat and bring soup to a simmer over medium-high. Add remaining 2 tablespoons butter, stirring to combine. Season with salt and pepper. Serve soup immediately, drizzled with pistachio oil and sprinkled with pistachio pieces.

GERMAN POTATO SALAD

Bacon fat is a crucial ingredient in true potato salad. It's blended with a bright vinaigrette to give the dish a delicious, multilayered flavor. Dress the potatoes when they're still warm—they'll better absorb the dressing. And make sure to cook the potatoes for only one minute under pressure so they remain firm.

—————————————— SERVES 6 ——————————————

3 pounds cooked potatoes (pages 86–87), drained

8 slices bacon, chopped

1 bunch scallions, cut crosswise into ½-inch pieces

½ cup Chicken, Vegetable, or Ham Stock, homemade (pages 24–26) or store-bought

¼ cup plus 2 tablespoons apple cider vinegar

3 tablespoons grainy mustard

Coarse salt and freshly ground pepper

½ cup chopped fresh flat-leaf parsley

1. Immediately after cooking potatoes, drain and return to pressure cooker; cover to keep warm.

2. Cook bacon in a skillet over medium heat until crisp, about 8 minutes. Using a slotted spoon, transfer bacon to a paper-towel–lined plate, leaving fat in skillet. Remove skillet from heat and add scallions. Let cool slightly. Add stock, vinegar, mustard, 1½ teaspoons salt, and ½ teaspoon pepper, and stir to combine.

3. In a large bowl, toss warm potatoes with dressing. Toss with parsley and reserved bacon, and serve.

BEET AND CITRUS SALAD WITH GREENS

A mix of earthy scarlet beets and slightly sweeter golden beets take well to the clean brightness of citrus. This dish keeps things simple—fresh orange and lemon zests flavor pressure-cooked beets, which are then dressed and tossed with greens. (We used kale, but try it also with arugula or dandelion greens.) It's wonderful as a lunch in winter, when citrus is in season and everyone needs a little vitamin C.

SERVES 6 TO 8

1 orange and 1 lemon, or 2 oranges

3 pounds cooked whole beets (pages 86–87), preferably red and golden, drained and cut into 1-inch wedges

4 ounces baby kale

3 tablespoons extra-virgin olive oil

Coarse salt and freshly ground pepper

Using a microplane zester, finely grate zest of orange and lemon; reserve for dressing. Cut ends from orange and lemon. Using a paring knife, remove peel and pith, following the curve of the fruit. Cut along membranes to remove segments. Toss citrus segments with beets, kale, oil, and reserved zests. Season with salt and pepper, and serve.

WARM CAULIFLOWER WITH PARSLEY AND CAPERS

Cauliflower's mildness practically begs for assertive ingredients to join forces with it. This salad heeds that call, with acidic vinegar and grainy mustard, salty capers, sweet shallots, and a generous helping of parsley at the finish. Remember the Pressure Principles (page 17) and cut the florets evenly in order to maintain texture.

SERVES 4 TO 6

- 2 tablespoons white wine vinegar
- 1 tablespoon finely chopped shallot
- 1 tablespoon capers, rinsed and drained
- 2 teaspoons grainy mustard

  Coarse salt and freshly ground pepper
- ¼ cup extra-virgin olive oil
- 2 pounds cooked cauliflower (pages 86–87), drained and kept warm
- ½ cup lightly packed fresh flat-leaf parsley, chopped

In a large shallow bowl, whisk together vinegar, shallot, capers, mustard, ½ teaspoon salt, and ½ teaspoon pepper. Slowly whisk in oil. Add warm cauliflower and parsley, and toss well to combine. Serve warm.

STEAMING allows cauliflower, broccoli—and all vegetables, ultimately—to retain more of their nutrients than cooking by other methods. Keep them warm in the cooker—just be sure to remove the lid in order to prevent overcooking.

BROCCOLI WITH LEMON-GARLIC VINAIGRETTE

At under a minute of steaming time, the pressure cooker allows for the quickest method for cooking broccoli. The vegetable is tender when pressure is reached, so turn off the machine immediately and allow the steam to vent quickly. (If you prefer your broccoli crisp, pressure-cooking is probably not the best method to use.) It doesn't take much to make broccoli sing—just a bit of fragrant garlic and a lemony vinaigrette.

SERVES 4 TO 6

3 tablespoons extra-virgin olive oil

2 garlic cloves, thinly sliced

1½ tablespoons fresh lemon juice

Coarse salt and freshly ground pepper

1¼ pounds cooked broccoli (pages 86–87), drained

1. Heat 1 tablespoon oil in a small skillet over medium. Add garlic and cook, stirring, until golden and fragrant, about 2 minutes. Transfer garlic to paper-towel-lined plate.

2. In a large shallow bowl, whisk together lemon juice, 1 teaspoon salt, and ½ teaspoon pepper. Slowly whisk in remaining 2 tablespoons oil. Add broccoli and reserved garlic, and toss to coat before serving.

WARM BUTTERNUT SQUASH SALAD WITH PUMPKIN SEEDS

Autumn produce offers ample opportunity for main-course salads. Here, pressure-cooked butternut squash is seasoned with a spiced vinaigrette, then scattered with pumpkin seeds, cilantro, and scallions. You can try this recipe with other winter squashes, too, such as delicata (which doesn't need to be peeled), acorn, and the versatile Long Island cheese pumpkin, one of the oldest American squash varieties. Be mindful of the brief time that the squash takes to cook; it can be perfectly tender after just a minute of pressure-cooking, depending on the size of the pieces.

—————————————— SERVES 4 TO 6 ——————————————

6 tablespoons plus 1 teaspoon extra-virgin olive oil

¼ cup pumpkin seeds

Coarse salt and freshly ground pepper

1 large garlic clove

3 tablespoons apple cider vinegar

1 teaspoon ground coriander

2 to 2½ pounds cooked butternut squash (pages 86–87), drained and kept warm

4 scallions (white and pale-green parts only), thinly sliced

Chopped fresh cilantro, for serving

1. Heat 1 teaspoon oil in a skillet over medium. Add pumpkin seeds; cook, stirring frequently, until seeds begin to brown and pop, 3 to 4 minutes. Remove from heat, and season with salt and pepper.

2. Chop garlic and add ½ teaspoon salt. Mash into a paste with the flat side of a knife; transfer to a small bowl. Add vinegar, coriander, and ½ teaspoon pepper, and whisk to combine. Slowly whisk in remaining 6 tablespoons oil.

3. Transfer warm butternut squash to a serving dish. Toss with dressing and top with pumpkin seeds, scallions, and cilantro.

CARROTS WITH WHOLE SPICES AND MAPLE

As an alternative to processed brown sugar in standard glazed carrots, substitute maple syrup for a subtle sweetness. This recipe also features a more interesting blend of whole spices than the usual ground varieties like cinnamon and nutmeg. The result is a more nuanced, much more contemporary side dish. If you prefer to cook the carrots whole, increase the pressure-cooking time to about 5 minutes, depending on the size of the carrots.

SERVES 6 TO 8

4 tablespoons unsalted butter

1 teaspoon fennel seeds

1 teaspoon yellow mustard seeds

1 teaspoon coriander seeds

Coarse salt and freshly ground pepper

2 tablespoons pure maple syrup

¼ cup snipped fresh chives

3 pounds cooked carrots (pages 86–87), drained and kept warm

Melt butter in a large skillet over medium-high heat. Add fennel seeds, mustard seeds, coriander seeds, 2 teaspoons salt, and ¾ teaspoon pepper. Cook, stirring frequently, until very fragrant, about 2 minutes. Remove skillet from heat and stir in maple syrup. Add warm dressing and chives to carrots, and toss to combine before serving.

BUTTERMILK MASHED POTATOES

MASHED BEETS WITH WASABI

MASHED BROCCOLI
WITH KALAMATA
OLIVES

MASHED CAULIFLOWER
WITH TURMERIC

MASHED BUTTERNUT SQUASH

MASHED BEETS WITH WASABI

Beets and horseradish are a celebrated pair. Here, wasabi, a root that is similar to horseradish but far more pungent, steps in to spike a lively beet mash. Dramatically red and deeply flavorful, it would make a fresh addition to your Thanksgiving plate. Beets are fairly fibrous, so reach for a blender instead of a food processor for the most velvety purée.

SERVES 6 TO 8

3 pounds cooked beets (pages 86–87), drained

¼ cup extra-virgin olive oil

2 to 3 tablespoons prepared wasabi paste, to taste

1 teaspoon finely grated fresh lemon zest, plus 1 tablespoon fresh juice

Coarse salt and freshly ground pepper

Sour cream, for garnish

Chopped fresh dill, for garnish

Purée beets, oil, wasabi, lemon zest and juice, 1 teaspoon salt, and ¼ teaspoon pepper in a blender or with an immersion blender until almost smooth, about 1 minute. Top with sour cream and dill, and serve.

BUTTERMILK MASHED POTATOES

You might think that potatoes would overcook in the pressure cooker. In fact, they become quite creamy—ideal for mashed potatoes. We love the way the mild sweetness of Yukon Gold potatoes plays off the tangy buttermilk in this mash. If you don't have buttermilk, substitute cream, half-and-half, milk, crème fraîche, or plain whole-milk yogurt.

SERVES 6 TO 8

3 pounds cooked Yukon Gold potatoes (pages 86–87), drained

¼ cup buttermilk

4 tablespoons unsalted butter

Coarse salt and freshly ground pepper

Snipped fresh chives, for garnish

Immediately after cooking potatoes, drain and return to pressure cooker; cover to keep warm. Add buttermilk, butter, 1 teaspoon salt, and ½ teaspoon pepper. Mash with a potato masher until smooth. Top with chives and serve.

MASHED BUTTERNUT SQUASH

The pressure cooker can quickly break down the fibers of winter squashes like butternut, resulting in the smoothest purées and mashes. Serve this mash with roast pork or duck. As an alternative to squash, root vegetables like carrots or sweet potatoes work equally well.

SERVES 4 TO 6

1 teaspoon extra-virgin olive oil

¼ cup pumpkin seeds, for garnish

Coarse salt and freshly ground pepper

2 pounds cooked butternut squash (pages 86–87), drained and kept warm

½ cup heavy cream

3 tablespoons unsalted butter

1. Heat oil in a skillet over medium. Add pumpkin seeds; cook, stirring frequently, until seeds begin to brown and pop, 3 to 4 minutes. Remove from heat, and season with salt and pepper.

2. Purée squash, cream, butter, and ½ teaspoon each salt and pepper in a food processor or blender until almost smooth. Season with more salt and pepper. Serve immediately, topped with pumpkin seeds.

MASHED BROCCOLI WITH KALAMATA OLIVES

In this rich green mash, lemon zest—a frequent companion to broccoli—teams up with Kalamata olives and garlic for a bright Mediterranean-inspired side. Serve this light, easy dish alongside roast chicken, lamb, or kebabs—or even toss with pasta.

SERVES 4 TO 6

1¼ pounds cooked broccoli (pages 86–87), drained and kept warm

2 tablespoons unsalted butter

8 Kalamata olives, pitted, plus more, slivered for garnish

Finely grated zest of 1 lemon

1 small garlic clove, finely chopped

Coarse salt and freshly ground pepper

Purée broccoli, butter, olives, zest, garlic, ½ teaspoon salt, and ¼ teaspoon pepper in a food processor until almost smooth. Season with salt and pepper. Serve topped with slivered olives.

MASHED CAULIFLOWER WITH TURMERIC

Infused with Indian spices, an otherwise ordinary cauliflower mash transforms into a golden, curried purée. Adding a single potato lends some heft, for a lovely alternative to mashed potatoes. Cook the two vegetables simultaneously—each takes only one minute—in the pressure cooker. For an authentic finish, cook some mustard seeds in vegetable (or mustard) oil over medium-high heat just until they pop, then drizzle the mixture over the mash.

—————————————— SERVES 4 TO 6 ——————————————

2 tablespoons unsalted butter

1 medium onion, finely chopped

1 teaspoon black mustard seeds

1 teaspoon coriander seeds

¼ teaspoon turmeric

2 pounds cooked cauliflower (pages 86–87), drained

1 medium cooked Yukon Gold potato (pages 86–87), drained

Coarse salt and freshly ground pepper

½ cup water

¼ cup chopped fresh cilantro, plus sprigs for garnish

1. Melt butter in a large pot over medium-low heat. Add onion, mustard seeds, coriander seeds, and turmeric, and cook, stirring, until onion is softened, about 6 minutes. Add cauliflower, potato, 1 teaspoon salt, and ½ teaspoon pepper, and stir to combine. Add the water and bring to a boil, stirring occasionally.

2. Transfer cauliflower mixture to a food processor or blender along with cilantro, and purée until almost smooth. Season with salt and pepper. Top with cilantro sprigs and serve.

MASHED CARROTS WITH CORIANDER

Coriander is used in two ways here: Ground seeds are blended into the carrot mash for a warm, citrusy effect, and coriander leaves, more commonly referred to as cilantro, are scattered over the top for a fresh finish. If you prefer, swap out the ground coriander for cumin, paprika (smoked would be nice here), or even curry powder. Keep this side dish in mind for a bright addition to a holiday table.

SERVES 6 TO 8

3 pounds cooked carrots (pages 86–87), plus 3 cups cooking liquid

4 tablespoons unsalted butter, softened

2 teaspoons ground coriander

Coarse salt and freshly ground pepper

Chopped fresh cilantro, for garnish

Warm carrots and reserved cooking liquid over medium-low heat, if necessary. Purée carrots and cooking liquid, butter, coriander, ¾ teaspoon salt, and ½ teaspoon pepper in a food processor or blender until smooth. Season with salt and pepper to taste. Top with cilantro and serve.

PART TWO

Hearty Mains & Sides

For many home cooks, the incredible value of the pressure cooker is that it can put a remarkable dinner on the table in next to no time flat. These are the dishes that help feed a family on even the most harried of weeknights, after a long day of school and work. You can walk through the door at, say, 6:00 and have a tasty, warm, seemingly long-cooked meal on the table by 7:00. But any of the following 40-plus recipes can just as easily serve as a memorable, company-worthy weekend meal, without hours of standing at the stove. Pork shoulder, for example, cooks so quickly and beautifully in the machine that we offer three outstanding variations. Just add a pot of potatoes or noodles, and dinner is done. Chicken and rice is a one-pot meal that takes kindly to the strengths of the pressure cooker: Here, you'll find Mexican, Indian, and Spanish adaptations of the comfort-food classic. Our list includes similar such favorites from around the world, all designed to keep you surprised and delighted—and most of all, satisfied.

PORK AND PINTO-BEAN CHILI

Keep this hearty Southwestern favorite in mind when you're expecting company, hosting a Super Bowl party, or just craving comfort food. Serve the smoky chili with cornbread or tortillas, diced white onion, pickled jalapeños, and sliced avocado.

SERVES 4

3 poblano chiles

3 tablespoons extra-virgin olive oil

1 pound boneless pork shoulder, cut into ¾-inch cubes

Coarse salt and freshly ground pepper

2 medium onions, finely chopped

3 garlic cloves, smashed

1½ teaspoons ground cumin

1 teaspoon dried oregano

2 dried bay leaves

3 tablespoons apple cider vinegar

7 or 8 cups Chicken Stock, homemade (page 24) or store-bought

2 cups dried pinto beans

1. Preheat broiler. Roast poblanos under broiler, turning, until completely charred, about 5 minutes. Transfer to a medium bowl; cover tightly with plastic wrap. Let sit for 10 minutes. Using your hands, rub off most of charred skin, rinsing hands frequently under cold running water. Slice poblanos in half, and remove ribs and seeds. Finely chop peppers.

2. Heat 2 tablespoons oil in a 6- to 8-quart stovetop pressure cooker over medium-high, or in an electric pressure cooker set to sauté. Season pork with salt and pepper. Add half the pork and cook, stirring occasionally, until browned, about 5 minutes; transfer to a plate. Repeat with remaining pork; transfer to plate.

3. Add remaining tablespoon oil, the onions, and garlic to pressure cooker, and cook, stirring occasionally, until softened, about 6 minutes. Add cumin, oregano, bay leaves, and poblanos, and cook, stirring, until combined, about 1 minute. Add vinegar, stock (8 cups for stovetop; 7 cups for electric), beans, reserved pork along with any accumulated juices, and 1 teaspoon salt, stirring up the browned bits, and bring to a boil.

4. **STOVETOP:** Secure lid. Bring to high pressure over medium-high heat; reduce heat to maintain pressure and cook for 26 minutes. Remove from heat, quickly release pressure (loosely cover vent with a clean kitchen towel), then remove lid.

    ELECTRIC: Secure lid. Manually set cooker to 31 minutes and let it come to pressure. Once time is complete, turn off, quickly release pressure (loosely cover vent with a clean kitchen towel), then remove lid.

5. Let pork and beans stand, uncovered, for 30 minutes in liquid. (Discard bay leaves.) Season with salt and pepper and serve.

CUBAN PORK SHOULDER

Mojo is a classic Cuban marinade (or sauce) that uses sour-orange juice and *lots* of garlic. Because sour oranges are not as easy to find in the States, we substituted fresh lime, grapefruit, and navel orange juices to achieve that same irresistible, slightly bittersweet tang. Serve the pork with steamed yellow rice, stewed black beans, and fried plantains.

SERVES 6 TO 8

- 1 tablespoon extra-virgin olive oil
- 1 bone-in pork shoulder (3 pounds)
- Coarse salt and freshly ground pepper
- ¾ cup fresh lime juice
- ½ cup fresh navel orange juice
- ½ cup fresh grapefruit juice
- 20 garlic cloves
- 1 tablespoon cumin seeds
- 5 marjoram or oregano sprigs, plus leaves for serving
- ¾ cup water (for stovetop pressure cooker only)

1. Heat oil in a 6- to 8-quart pressure cooker over high, or in an electric pressure cooker set to sauté. Pat pork dry, and season with 1 teaspoon salt and ½ teaspoon pepper. Cook pork, turning, until browned on all sides, about 10 minutes. Add lime juice, orange juice, grapefruit juice, garlic, cumin, marjoram sprigs, and 1 teaspoon salt. If using a stovetop pressure cooker, add the water.

2. **STOVETOP:** Secure lid. Bring to high pressure over medium-high heat; reduce heat to maintain pressure and cook for 50 minutes. Remove from heat, quickly release pressure, then remove lid.

   ELECTRIC: Secure lid. Manually set cooker to 50 minutes and let it come to pressure. Once time is complete, turn off, quickly release pressure, then remove lid.

3. Let pork stand in cooking liquid for 10 minutes. Skim any fat from surface. Transfer pork to a cutting board and slice. Top with marjoram leaves and serve with sauce.

Allow the pork to **ABSORB THE SAUCE** by letting the meat stand in the cooking liquid for 10 minutes after cooking.

WINE-BRAISED PORK SHOULDER

Pork pairs especially well with sweet, fruity flavors. This recipe takes full advantage of that with a combination of dried apricots, prunes, and cranberries and a generous measure of red wine. Feel free to experiment with other combinations of fruits (figs, raisins, and cherries are another great mix). In testing, we liked the pressure-cooked Ham Stock (page 25) best in this "braise," but you can use more readily available chicken stock in its place. (Since the chicken stock is less salty, you may need to taste and adjust the seasoning.)

SERVES 6 TO 8

- 1 tablespoon extra-virgin olive oil
- 1 bone-in pork shoulder (3 pounds)

  Coarse salt and freshly ground pepper

- 1 large onion, thinly sliced
- ¼ cup finely chopped peeled fresh ginger
- 1 cup dry red wine
- 1½ or 2½ cups Ham or Chicken Stock, homemade (page 25 or 24) or store-bought
- 2 cups mixed dried fruit, such as apricots, prunes, and cranberries

1. Heat oil in a 6- to 8-quart stovetop pressure cooker over high, or in an electric pressure cooker set to sauté. Pat pork dry, and season with 1 teaspoon salt and ½ teaspoon pepper. Add pork and cook, turning, until browned on all sides, about 10 minutes; transfer to a plate. Add onion and ginger, and cook, stirring occasionally, until softened, about 5 minutes. Stir in wine and cook until reduced by half, about 5 minutes. Add stock (2½ cups for stovetop; 1½ cups for electric) and dried fruit. Return pork to pressure cooker along with any accumulated juices.

2. **STOVETOP:** Secure lid. Bring to high pressure over medium-high heat; reduce heat to maintain pressure and cook for 50 minutes. Remove from heat, quickly release pressure, then remove lid.

   ELECTRIC: Secure lid. Manually set cooker to 50 minutes and let it come to pressure. Once time is complete, turn off, quickly release pressure, then remove lid.

3. Let pork stand in cooking liquid for 10 minutes. Skim any fat from surface. Transfer pork to a cutting board and slice. Serve with braised fruit.

PORK SHOULDER STEW

1 tablespoon extra-virgin olive oil

1 bone-in pork shoulder (3 pounds)

Coarse salt and freshly ground pepper

1 large leek (white and pale-green parts only), rinsed well and thinly sliced

1 medium carrot, diced

1 celery stalk, thinly sliced

1 cup dry white wine

1½ or 2½ cups water, plus 1 tablespoon cold water

1 ounce dried mushrooms, such as porcini or oyster

2 tablespoons pure maple syrup

1 tablespoon Dijon mustard

1 tablespoon grainy mustard

1 teaspoon caraway seeds

1 dried bay leaf

1 teaspoon cornstarch

⅓ cup heavy cream

Chopped fresh dill, for garnish

This variation on pork shoulder was inspired by French stews, with a combination of Dijon and grainy mustards, but sweetened with a touch of maple syrup, a distinctly North American ingredient. Serve it over egg noodles or with a side of buttered dill potatoes.

—————————————— SERVES 6 TO 8 ——————————————

1. Heat oil in a 6- to 8-quart pressure cooker over high, or in an electric pressure cooker set to sauté. Pat pork dry, and season with 1 teaspoon salt and ½ teaspoon pepper. Cook pork, turning, until browned on all sides, about 10 minutes; transfer pork to a plate. Add leek, carrot, celery, and 1 teaspoon salt, and cook, stirring occasionally, until leek has softened, about 5 minutes. Add wine and cook until reduced by half. Stir in water (2½ cups for stovetop; 1½ cups for electric), mushrooms, maple syrup, both mustards, caraway seeds, and bay leaf. Return pork to pressure cooker along with any accumulated juices.

2. **STOVETOP:** Secure lid. Bring to high pressure over medium-high heat; reduce heat to maintain pressure and cook for 50 minutes. Remove from heat, quickly release pressure, then remove lid.

   ELECTRIC: Secure lid. Manually set cooker to 50 minutes and let it come to pressure. Once time is complete, turn off, quickly release pressure, then remove lid.

3. Let pork stand in cooking liquid for 10 minutes. Skim any fat from surface. Transfer pork to a cutting board and pull meat from bones.

4. Meanwhile, bring remaining cooking liquid to a boil over high heat or using the sauté function. (Discard bay leaf.) In a small bowl, combine cornstarch and remaining tablespoon water. Stir cornstarch mixture into cooking liquid and boil until thickened, about 1 minute. Stir in cream, and season with salt and pepper. Return pork to sauce along with any accumulated juices. Serve stew topped with dill.

ALABAMA-STYLE PULLED PORK

Alabama barbecue sauce has a key ingredient that keeps the meat rich and moist: mayonnaise. Meanwhile, the vinegar helps to tenderize and adds tanginess. We put a spin on the sauce by adding spices like cumin and coriander, and utilized the pressure cooker to make quick(er) work of a long-cooked pork shoulder—done in less than two hours instead of four. The result is something totally new and yet familiar at once. Serve the pork with sandwich bread, buns, or steamed white rice.

SERVES 6 TO 8

1 bone-in pork shoulder (5 to 6 pounds)

Coarse salt and freshly ground pepper

2 or 4 cups water

½ cup distilled white vinegar

¼ cup Worcestershire sauce

¼ cup grainy mustard

¼ cup honey

1 teaspoon hot sauce

1 teaspoon sweet smoked paprika

1 teaspoon ground cumin

1 teaspoon ground coriander

½ cup mayonnaise

1. Heat a 6- to 8-quart stovetop pressure cooker over high, or set an electric pressure cooker to sauté. Pat pork dry, and season with 1 teaspoon salt and ½ teaspoon pepper. Add pork, fat side down, and cook, turning, until browned on both sides, about 10 minutes. Add water (4 cups for stovetop; 2 cups for electric), vinegar, Worcestershire, mustard, honey, hot sauce, smoked paprika, cumin, coriander, and 1 teaspoon salt.

2. **STOVETOP:** Secure lid. Bring to high pressure over medium-high heat; reduce heat to maintain pressure and cook for 80 minutes. Remove from heat, quickly release pressure, then remove lid.

   ELECTRIC: Secure lid. Manually set cooker to 90 minutes and let it come to pressure. Once time is complete, turn off, quickly release pressure, then remove lid.

3. Let pork stand in cooking liquid for 10 minutes. Skim any fat from surface. Transfer pork to a cutting board. Whisk mayonnaise into cooking liquid. Slice pork or pull meat from bones; return meat to sauce along with any accumulated juices. Season with salt and pepper and serve.

ALSATIAN-STYLE PORK RIBS

Pork and sauerkraut (*choucroute*) are hallmarks of the hearty cooking of Alsace, in northeastern France. Spare ribs (from the belly) and country-style ribs (from the blade end of the loin) have enough fat on them to withstand pressure-cooking and stay juicy and tender. Country-style ribs have more meat and fat; spare ribs have more bone. Depending on how you like them (some prefer fork-tender ribs; others like a little chew), you can increase or decrease the half-hour cooking time by five minutes.

SERVES 4 TO 6

---

1 tablespoon extra-virgin olive oil

1 rack pork spare ribs or country-style ribs (3 pounds), cut into 2 pieces

Coarse salt and freshly ground pepper

3 tablespoons unsalted butter

2 medium onions, halved lengthwise and thinly sliced

1 cup dry white wine

1 cup water (for stovetop pressure cooker only)

8 ounces crème fraîche

2 pounds sauerkraut (about 4 cups), rinsed and drained

3 tablespoons dark brown sugar

1. Heat oil in a 6- to 8-quart stovetop pressure cooker over medium-high, or in an electric pressure cooker set to sauté. Season pork with 1 teaspoon salt and ½ teaspoon pepper. Add 1 piece pork to pressure cooker, meat side down, and cook until browned, about 5 minutes; transfer to a plate. Repeat with remaining pork and transfer to plate. Add butter and onions, and cook, stirring occasionally, until golden, about 6 minutes. Stir in wine, the water if using a stovetop pressure cooker, and crème fraîche, scraping up any browned bits. Add sauerkraut and sugar. Return pork to pressure cooker along with any accumulated juices.

2. **STOVETOP:** Secure lid. Bring to high pressure over medium-high heat; reduce heat to maintain pressure and cook for 30 minutes. Remove from heat, quickly release pressure, then remove lid.

   ELECTRIC: Secure lid. Manually set cooker to 30 minutes and let it come to pressure. Once time is complete, turn off, quickly release pressure, then remove lid.

3. Let pork stand in cooking liquid for 10 minutes. Skim any fat from surface. Transfer pork to a cutting board and cut between each rib to separate. Serve with sauerkraut.

COLOMBIAN CHICKEN AND POTATO STEW

3 tablespoons unsalted butter

1 large white onion, finely chopped

5 cups Chicken Stock, homemade (page 24) or store-bought

4 bone-in, skin-on chicken thighs

2 small bone-in, skin-on chicken breast halves

2 medium russet potatoes, peeled and coarsely grated

1 pound small yellow potatoes, such as baby Yukon Gold, scrubbed

2 teaspoons dried oregano, crumbled

Coarse salt and freshly ground pepper

2 cups fresh corn kernels, sliced off the cob, or frozen

1 cup heavy cream

3 tablespoons capers, rinsed and drained

2 large avocados, halved, pitted, peeled, and chopped, for garnish

Fresh cilantro, for garnish

Lime wedges, for serving

This soup-stew (known as *ajiaco*) traditionally employs *guasca*, an aromatic herb native to Colombia, but cilantro makes a satisfying substitute. Small, yellow potatoes, *papas criollas*, break down during cooking to create an ultra-rich broth—if you have access to a Latin market, look for them. We used potatoes that are readily available: russet, a starchy potato that we grated to produce a silky broth, and Yukon Gold, a waxier potato that holds its shape for a nicely textured stew. If corn is in season, you can substitute fresh cobs, cut into 1- to 2-inch rounds, for the kernels.

——————————— SERVES 6 ———————————

1. Melt butter in a 6- to 8-quart stovetop pressure cooker over medium heat, or in an electric pressure cooker set to sauté. Cook onion, stirring, until softened, about 5 minutes. Add stock, chicken thighs and breasts, russet and yellow potatoes, oregano, 1½ teaspoons salt, and ¾ teaspoon pepper.

2. **STOVETOP:** Secure lid. Bring to high pressure over medium-high heat; reduce heat to maintain pressure and cook for 15 minutes. Remove from heat, quickly release pressure, then remove lid. Transfer chicken to a rimmed baking sheet and let cool slightly. Return cooker to medium heat.

   ELECTRIC: Secure lid. Manually set cooker to 20 minutes and let it come to pressure. Once time is complete, turn off, quickly release pressure, then remove lid. Transfer chicken to a rimmed baking sheet and let cool slightly. Set cooker to sauté.

3. Add corn, cream, and capers to pressure cooker, and bring to a simmer. Cook until heated through, about 2 minutes.

4. Using two forks, shred chicken (discard skin and bones); return to cooker. Season with salt and pepper. Top with avocado and cilantro, and serve with lime wedges.

ARROZ CON POLLO

Chicken and rice is a one-pot wonder whose flavor profile can be easily customized. Take *arroz con pollo*: Some versions use saffron; we rely on annatto paste for the distinctive tang and yellow-orange hue. Made with annatto seeds and spices, the paste is used throughout Mexico in rubs, sauces, and marinades.

SERVES 4 TO 6

3 tablespoons extra-virgin olive oil

3 pounds bone-in, skin-on chicken drumsticks and thighs (8 to 10 pieces)

1 large onion, finely chopped

1 green bell pepper, ribs and seeds removed, finely chopped

1 red bell pepper, ribs and seeds removed, finely chopped

3 large garlic cloves, minced

2 tablespoons annatto paste (we like El Yucateco)

Coarse salt

3 cups water

1½ cups long-grain white rice

¼ cup pitted green olives, quartered if large

Fresh cilantro leaves, for garnish (optional)

1. Heat oil in a 6- to 8-quart stovetop pressure cooker over medium-high, or in an electric pressure cooker set to sauté. Add chicken, skin side down, and cook until golden brown, flipping halfway through, about 8 minutes total; transfer to a plate.

2. Add onion, green and red bell peppers, and garlic to cooker, and cook, stirring, until softened, 5 to 8 minutes. Crumble in annatto paste and add 1½ teaspoons salt. Cook, stirring, 1 minute. Return chicken to cooker along with any accumulated juices, and turn to coat with vegetables. Stir in the water and bring to a boil. Stir in rice and olives.

3. **STOVETOP:** Secure lid. Bring to high pressure over medium-high heat; reduce heat to maintain pressure and cook for 10 minutes. Remove from heat and let pressure decrease naturally for 5 minutes. Release remaining pressure (loosely cover vent with a clean kitchen towel), then remove lid.

   ELECTRIC: Manually set cooker to 12 minutes and let it come to pressure. Once time is complete, turn off, quickly release pressure (loosely cover vent with a clean kitchen towel), then remove lid. If rice isn't fully tender, close lid to let rice continue to steam, 5 to 10 minutes.

4. Top with cilantro leaves, if desired, and serve.

INDIAN-SPICED CHICKEN AND RICE

1 tablespoon vegetable oil

3 pounds bone-in, skinless chicken thighs

1 large leek, rinsed well and thinly sliced

¼ cup finely chopped peeled fresh ginger

5 garlic cloves, smashed

Coarse salt and freshly ground pepper

1 tablespoon mustard seeds

1 tablespoon coriander seeds

1 tablespoon cumin seeds

1 tablespoon curry powder

1 tablespoon chili powder, preferably Kashmiri

1 can (35 ounces) crushed tomatoes, blended

1 cup water

1 small head cauliflower (6 to 8 ounces), cut into florets

1½ cups basmati rice

Chopped fresh dill, for garnish (optional)

Plain whole-milk yogurt, for serving

Cauliflower and tomatoes turn this dish of spiced chicken thighs and basmati rice into a complete meal. The juice from the tomatoes combines with water to keep the rice from drying out under pressure. To add a touch of heat and a vibrant red color, we used Kashmiri chili powder, which is a bit milder than traditional chili powder.

——————— **SERVES 4 TO 6** ———————

1. Heat oil in a 6- to 8-quart stovetop pressure cooker over medium-high, or in an electric pressure cooker set to sauté. Add chicken and cook, turning once, until golden brown, about 8 minutes; transfer to a plate. Add leek, ginger, garlic, and 1 teaspoon salt to pressure cooker, and cook, stirring, until softened and golden, 6 to 8 minutes. Add mustard, coriander, and cumin seeds, and cook, stirring occasionally, until fragrant, about 2 minutes. Add curry and chili powders and cook, stirring, until fragrant, about 30 seconds. Add reserved chicken, the tomatoes, the water, cauliflower, 2 teaspoons salt, and 1 teaspoon pepper. Bring to a boil, then add rice.

2. **STOVETOP:** Secure lid. Bring to high pressure over medium-high heat; reduce heat to maintain pressure and cook for 10 minutes. Remove from heat, quickly release pressure (loosely cover vent with a clean kitchen towel), then remove lid.

   ELECTRIC: Secure lid. Manually set cooker to 15 minutes and let it come to pressure. Once time is complete, turn off, quickly release pressure (loosely cover vent with a clean kitchen towel), then remove lid.

3. Top with dill, if desired, and serve with yogurt.

CILANTRO CHICKEN AND RICE

Cubanelle and serrano chiles bring a balance of mild sweetness and spicy heat to this Mexican-inspired meal. Blended with herbs and spices, they form a fragrant sauce that beautifully infuses the chicken as it pressure-cooks. You can brighten the dish even further with a bit of grated fresh ginger or with tomatoes in summer (the amount of cooking liquid remains the same).

_____ SERVES 4 TO 6 _____

1 medium bunch fresh cilantro, plus more for garnish

½ cup finely chopped white onion

3 garlic cloves

1 cubanelle or poblano chile, stemmed and seeded

1 serrano chile, seeds and ribs removed, if desired

1 teaspoon dried oregano

1 teaspoon cumin seeds

5 allspice berries or ¼ teaspoon ground allspice

Coarse salt and freshly ground pepper

1½ to 2 cups water

3 pounds bone-in, skinless chicken thighs

1½ cups long-grain rice

Lime wedges, for serving

1. In a blender, purée cilantro, onion, garlic, both chiles, oregano, cumin seeds, allspice, 1 teaspoon salt, 1 teaspoon pepper, and ½ cup water. Add enough water (remaining 1 to 1½ cups) to measure a total of 3 cups liquid. Transfer cilantro mixture to a 6- to 8-quart pressure cooker.

2. **STOVETOP:** Add chicken and bring to a boil over medium-high heat. Add rice and stir to combine. Secure lid. Bring to high pressure over medium-high heat; reduce heat to maintain pressure and cook for 10 minutes. Remove from heat, quickly release pressure (loosely cover vent with a clean kitchen towel), then remove lid.

   ELECTRIC: Add chicken and bring to a boil using the sauté function. Add rice and stir to combine. Secure lid. Manually set cooker to 15 minutes and let it come to pressure. Once time is complete, turn off, quickly release pressure (loosely cover vent with a clean kitchen towel), then remove lid.

3. Top with cilantro or other fresh herbs and serve with lime wedges.

COQ AU VIN

6 large garlic cloves, 3 smashed and 3 minced

4 black peppercorns

1 dried bay leaf

2 thyme sprigs, plus leaves for garnish

7 flat-leaf parsley sprigs, stems and leaves separated

8 bone-in, skin-on chicken thighs (about 3 pounds)

Coarse salt and freshly ground pepper

All-purpose flour

1 tablespoon unsalted butter

2 tablespoons extra-virgin olive oil

12 ounces white mushrooms, halved

8 ounces pearl onions, peeled

3 tablespoons cognac

¾ cup dry red wine

2¼ or 2¾ cups Chicken Stock, homemade (page 24) or store-bought

1 tablespoon tomato paste

Traditionally, this French bistro classic involves braising chicken slowly in red wine. But when coq au vin is made in the pressure cooker, the deeply satisfying flavor is equal to that of traditional stovetop simmering—in about a third of the time. Serve it with smashed potatoes or noodles for a dish that's sure to satisfy.

———————— SERVES 6 ————————

1. Using a piece of cheesecloth, make a bouquet garni: Wrap smashed garlic cloves, the peppercorns, bay leaf, thyme sprigs, and parsley stems; tie with kitchen twine. Season chicken with salt and pepper. Place flour in a shallow dish and dredge chicken, shaking off excess.

2. Heat butter and 1 tablespoon oil in a 6- to 8-quart stovetop pressure cooker over medium, or in an electric pressure cooker set to sauté. Working in batches, cook chicken until golden brown on both sides, 3 to 4 minutes; transfer to a plate.

3. Add remaining oil and increase heat to medium-high. Add mushrooms, onions, and minced garlic. Season with salt and pepper. Cook until golden, about 6 minutes; transfer to a plate.

4. Add cognac and wine. Using a wooden spoon, scrape up any browned bits, and cook until reduced by half, about 4 minutes. Add stock (2¾ cups for stovetop; 2¼ cups for electric), tomato paste, bouquet garni, and reserved chicken; bring to a boil.

5. **STOVETOP:** Secure lid. Bring to high pressure over medium-high heat; reduce heat to maintain pressure and cook for 10 minutes. Remove from heat, quickly release pressure, then remove lid. With a slotted spoon, transfer chicken, mushrooms, and onions to a bowl. (Discard bouquet garni.) Return cooker to medium-high heat.

   ELECTRIC: Secure lid. Manually set cooker to 14 minutes and let it come to pressure. Once time is complete, turn off, quickly release pressure, then remove lid. With a slotted spoon, transfer chicken, mushrooms, and onions to a bowl. (Discard bouquet garni.) Set cooker to sauté.

6. Bring to a boil and cook until liquid is reduced by half, about 7 minutes. Return chicken, mushrooms, and onions to cooker and cook for 2 minutes. Skim any fat from surface, and season with salt. Stir in parsley leaves, top with thyme leaves, and serve.

TURKEY MEATBALLS IN BÉCHAMEL SAUCE

1¼ pounds ground turkey

1 cup plain panko (Japanese breadcrumbs)

1 small onion, finely chopped

2 large eggs, lightly beaten

2 tablespoons finely chopped fresh flat-leaf parsley leaves

1 teaspoon finely chopped fresh thyme leaves

1 teaspoon sweet paprika

½ teaspoon freshly grated nutmeg

Coarse salt and freshly ground pepper

4½ cups whole milk

3 tablespoons extra-virgin olive oil

4 tablespoons unsalted butter

½ cup all-purpose flour

Chopped fresh dill, for garnish

Turkey meatballs turn out extra juicy in a pressure cooker. The larger flakes of panko help keep the meatballs crisper and lighter than traditional breadcrumbs, but use whatever you have available. Because ground turkey is less dense and less fatty than ground beef, refrigerating the meatballs before browning helps them set and hold together better as they cook in the creamy béchamel sauce. Serve with egg noodles and a simple green salad.

—————— MAKES 20 MEATBALLS ——————

1. In a large bowl, mix together turkey, panko, onion, eggs, parsley, thyme, paprika, nutmeg, 1½ teaspoons salt, ½ teaspoon pepper, and ½ cup milk until well combined. With damp hands or an ice-cream scoop, form mixture into 1½-inch balls, transferring to a rimmed baking sheet as you work. Refrigerate at least 1 hour or, covered, up to overnight.

2. Heat 1½ tablespoons oil in a 6- to 8-quart pressure cooker over medium-high, or in an electric pressure cooker set to sauté. Add half the meatballs and cook until browned on all sides, about 5 minutes; transfer to a plate. Repeat with remaining oil and meatballs. Melt butter in pressure cooker, then stir in flour. Whisk in remaining 4 cups milk, ½ teaspoon salt, and ½ teaspoon pepper. Return meatballs to pressure cooker.

3. **STOVETOP:** Secure lid. Bring to high pressure over medium-high heat; reduce heat to maintain pressure and cook for 4 minutes. Remove from heat, quickly release pressure, then remove lid.

   ELECTRIC: Secure lid. Manually set cooker to 4 minutes and let it come to pressure. Once time is complete, turn off, quickly release pressure, then remove lid.

4. Top with dill and serve.

BRAISED DUCK WITH TURNIPS AND CELERY ROOT

Duck is a prime candidate for the pressure cooker; its richness and ample juices intensify the ingredients that share the pot with it—in this case, sturdy root vegetables. Use the tasty duck fat to fry up sage leaves for a crisp finishing touch.

SERVES 6

- 6 duck legs, trimmed of excess fat

  Coarse salt and freshly ground pepper

- 2 small onions, halved lengthwise and cut into thin wedges

- 3 large garlic cloves, smashed

- 2 cups dry white wine

- 1 pound turnips, peeled and cut into 1-inch-thick wedges

- 1½ pounds celery root, peeled and cut into 1-inch-thick wedges

- 2 dried bay leaves

- 1 bunch fresh sage

  Extra-virgin olive oil, if needed

1. Heat a 6- to 8-quart stovetop pressure cooker over medium-high, or in an electric pressure cooker to sauté. Pat duck dry and season with 1 teaspoon salt and ½ teaspoon pepper. Working in two batches, cook legs, skin side down, turning once, until browned, 10 to 12 minutes per batch; transfer legs to a plate. Remove all but 2 tablespoons duck fat from pressure cooker and reserve for frying sage leaves. Add onions and garlic, and cook, stirring, until softened, about 3 minutes. Add wine, turnips, celery root, bay leaves, and 2 sage sprigs. Return duck to pressure cooker along with any accumulated juices.

2. **STOVETOP:** Secure lid. Bring to high pressure over medium-high heat; reduce heat to maintain pressure and cook for 20 minutes. Remove from heat, quickly release pressure, then remove lid.

   ELECTRIC: Secure lid. Manually set cooker to 25 minutes and let it come to pressure. Once time is complete, turn off, quickly release pressure, then remove lid.

3. Meanwhile, fry sage leaves. Place excess duck fat in a small skillet (you should have about 1 cup; if not, add olive oil to equal 1 cup) and heat over medium until hot, about 3 minutes. Separate sage leaves from sprigs and fry a few at a time, turning once, until crisp but not brown (if they are browning, turn down the heat), about 1 minute; transfer to a paper-towel–lined plate and season with salt.

4. Transfer duck and vegetables to plates, and serve topped with fried sage leaves.

BEEF BORSCHT

1 teaspoon caraway seeds

Coarse salt and freshly ground pepper

2½ pounds beef chuck or shin, cut into 2-inch pieces

1 pound bone-in beef short-ribs, cut into 3-inch sections, if necessary

3 tablespoons extra-virgin olive oil

2 cups water

1 can (28 ounces) whole tomatoes

3 large beets (1½ pounds), peeled and coarsely grated

½ small green cabbage (about 1 pound), shredded

1 large carrot, peeled and coarsely grated

1 medium onion, chopped

1 small green bell pepper, ribs and seeds removed, chopped

1 tablespoon red-wine vinegar

Sour cream and chopped fresh dill, for serving

Borscht is such a time-honored Eastern European recipe, but some cooks find the delicious beet-centric soup too labor-intensive. Not with the pressure cooker, which lets you avoid boiling or roasting the beets separately or sautéing the other vegetables. Grating the beets beforehand helps them dissolve into the broth to maximize flavor (which is also given a boost with well-marbled beef chuck and bone-in short ribs).

——————————— SERVES 8 ———————————

1. Grind caraway seeds in a coffee or spice grinder; transfer to a small bowl. Add 2 teaspoons salt and 1 teaspoon pepper. Pat beef dry and rub with caraway mixture.

2. Heat oil in a 6- to 8-quart stovetop pressure cooker over medium-high, or in an electric pressure cooker set to sauté. Working in batches, cook beef until browned on all sides, about 5 minutes per batch; transfer to a plate. Return beef with any accumulated juices to cooker. Add the water, tomatoes (with their juices), beets, cabbage, carrot, onion, bell pepper, and vinegar.

3. **STOVETOP:** Secure lid. Bring to high pressure over medium-high heat; reduce heat to maintain pressure and cook for 45 minutes. Remove from heat, quickly release pressure, then remove lid.

   ELECTRIC: Secure lid. Manually set cooker to 45 minutes and let it come to pressure. Once time is complete, turn off, quickly release pressure, then remove lid.

4. Transfer beef to a cutting board and pull meat from bones; return meat to soup. Skim fat from surface. Season borscht with salt and pepper, and serve with sour cream and dill.

DIJON AND TOMATO BEEF STEW

A bowl of beef stew can take the chill off even the most wintery day. This one employs tangy Dijon mustard to unite the other ingredients—beef chuck, onions, mushrooms, carrots, and tomatoes. You can make it a meal by serving it with mashed potatoes or crusty bread, some greens, and a bottle of red wine such as Cabernet or Zinfandel.

————————————— **SERVES 6** —————————————

- 2 tablespoons extra-virgin olive oil
- 3 pounds boneless beef chuck, cut into 1½-inch cubes

  Coarse salt and freshly ground pepper
- 2 or 4 cups water
- 1 pound white mushrooms, trimmed and halved or quartered if large
- 2 medium onions, finely chopped
- 1 medium carrot, finely chopped
- 1 celery stalk, finely chopped
- 2 garlic cloves, coarsely chopped
- 1 can (28 ounces) whole tomatoes
- ¼ cup Dijon mustard

  Sliced fresh basil, for garnish (optional)

1. Heat oil in 6- to 8-quart stovetop pressure cooker over medium-high, or in an electric pressure cooker set to sauté. Pat beef dry and season with 1½ teaspoons salt and ¾ teaspoon pepper. Working in batches, cook beef until browned on all sides, 6 to 8 minutes; transfer to a plate.

2. Add 1 cup water to pressure cooker, scraping up browned bits with a wooden spoon. Add 3 cups more water for stovetop, and 1 cup more water for electric. Add mushrooms, onions, carrot, celery, garlic, tomatoes (with their juices), mustard, and ½ teaspoon salt. Return beef to pressure cooker along with any accumulated juices.

3. **STOVETOP:** Secure lid. Bring to high pressure over medium-high heat; reduce heat to maintain pressure and cook for 60 minutes. Remove from heat, quickly release pressure, then remove lid.

   ELECTRIC: Secure lid. Manually set cooker to 60 minutes and let it come to pressure. Once time is complete, turn off, quickly release pressure, then remove lid.

4. Skim any fat from the surface. Top stew with basil, if desired, and serve.

MISO-APRICOT SHORT RIBS

We love the way the pressure cooker promotes silky, falling-off-the-bone texture for braise-worthy cuts like short ribs and brisket. Bone-in ribs take slightly longer than boneless ones, but we find the flavor worth the wait. Here, the ribs are paired with an inspired combination of ingredients (miso paste, whole coriander seeds, and apricots, among them) for a dish that's easy—but memorable enough for special occasions. Serve over mashed potatoes or with rice.

SERVES 6 TO 8

4 pounds bone-in beef short ribs

Coarse salt and freshly ground pepper

4 garlic cloves, smashed

¼ cup all-purpose flour

1 cup marsala or fino sherry

3 cups Chicken Stock, homemade (page 24) or store-bought, or water

1 cup chopped dried apricots

⅓ cup white miso

1 tablespoon coriander seeds

2 scallions, thinly sliced on a diagonal, for serving

Peeled fresh ginger, thinly sliced into matchsticks, for serving (optional)

1. Heat a 6- to 8-quart stovetop pressure cooker over medium-high, or set an electric pressure cooker to sauté. Pat ribs dry and season with 1 teaspoon salt and ½ teaspoon pepper. Working in batches, add ribs, fat side down, and cook until browned on all sides, 8 to 10 minutes; transfer to a plate. Pour out all but 2 tablespoons fat from pressure cooker. Add garlic and flour and cook, stirring, until fragrant, 1 to 2 minutes. Stir in marsala, stock, apricots, miso, coriander seeds, 1 teaspoon salt, and ½ teaspoon pepper. Return ribs to pressure cooker along with any accumulated juices.

2. **STOVETOP:** Secure lid. Bring to high pressure over medium-high heat; reduce heat to maintain pressure and cook for 60 minutes. Remove from heat, quickly release pressure, then remove lid.

   ELECTRIC: Secure lid. Manually set cooker to 60 minutes and let it come to pressure. Once time is complete, turn off, quickly release pressure, then remove lid.

3. Let ribs stand in liquid for 10 minutes. Transfer to a cutting board and cut between each rib to separate. Transfer to a serving platter. Spoon sauce over meat, top with sliced scallions and ginger (if desired), and serve.

POT ROAST WITH DATES, OLIVES, AND ORANGE

With a pressure cooker, the classic Sunday afternoon pot roast can be on the table in under two hours—without ever turning on your oven. We seasoned this one with North African ingredients, but remained loyal to the traditional American chuck roast, which, like other inexpensive cuts, braises well. If your chuck roast has enough fat on it, you can omit the oil for searing. Serve with potatoes (mashed or boiled and buttered), egg noodles, or couscous.

SERVES 6 TO 8

- 1 tablespoon extra-virgin olive oil
- 1 boneless beef chuck roast (about 3 pounds)
- Coarse salt and freshly ground pepper
- 2 garlic cloves, smashed
- 2 tablespoons all-purpose flour
- 3 cups Chicken Stock, homemade (page 24) or store-bought
- 1 pound carrots, cut into thick rounds
- ⅓ cup pitted oil-cured olives
- 10 dates, pitted and chopped
- 1 teaspoon fresh thyme leaves
- 1 dried bay leaf
- ½ teaspoon cumin seeds
- Finely grated zest and juice of 1 large navel orange

1. Heat oil in a 6- to 8-quart pressure cooker over medium-high, or in an electric pressure cooker set to sauté. Pat beef dry and season with 1 teaspoon salt and ½ teaspoon pepper. Add beef and cook until browned on all sides, 8 to 10 minutes; transfer to a plate. Pour out all but 2 tablespoons fat (or add enough oil to equal 2 tablespoons). Add garlic and flour, and cook, stirring, until fragrant, 1 to 2 minutes. Whisk in stock, carrots, olives, dates, thyme, bay leaf, cumin seeds, orange zest and juice, and 1 teaspoon salt. Return beef along with any accumulated juices to pressure cooker.

2. **STOVETOP:** Secure lid. Bring to high pressure over medium-high heat; reduce heat to maintain pressure and cook for 60 minutes. Remove from heat, quickly release pressure, then remove lid.

   ELECTRIC: Secure lid. Manually set cooker to 90 minutes and let it come to pressure. Once time is complete, turn off, quickly release pressure, then remove lid.

3. Let beef stand in liquid for 10 minutes. Skim any fat from surface. Transfer beef to a serving platter. (Discard bay leaf.) Spoon sauce over and around beef and serve.

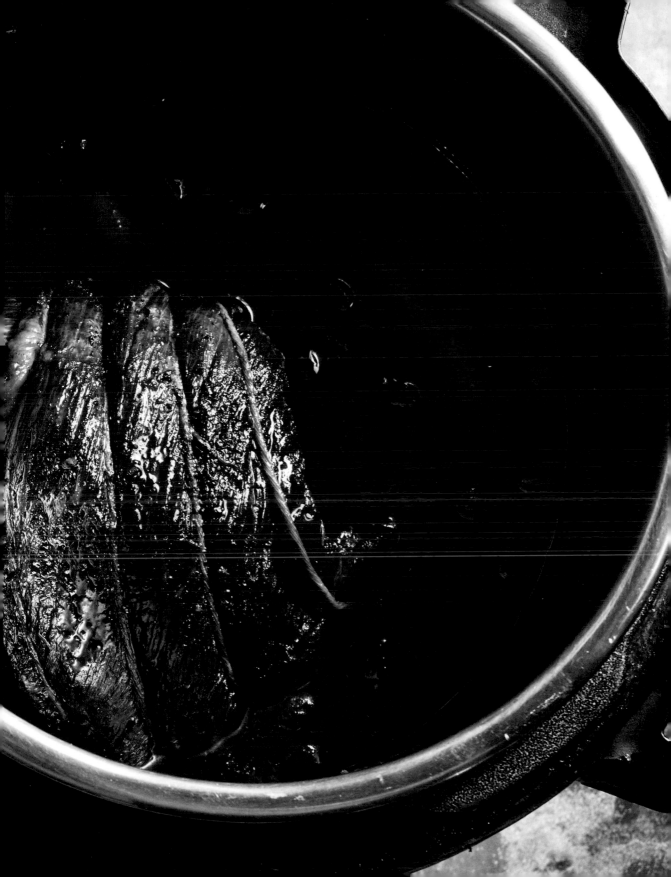

SLOPPY JOES

There are plenty of stories about how the sloppy joe got its name—from a Cuban bar, from a diner in Sioux City, Iowa—but one sure thing is that this sweet-tangy ground beef sandwich is an all-American favorite. Our version dispenses with the usual ketchup or chili sauce in favor of crushed tomatoes, chili powder, and maple syrup. Just don't forget the napkins.

—————————————— SERVES 6 ——————————————

2 tablespoons unsalted butter

½ pound ground beef (85 percent lean)

½ pound ground pork

½ pound ground veal

Coarse salt and freshly ground pepper

1 medium onion, finely chopped

1 medium red bell pepper, ribs and seeds removed, chopped

1 celery stalk, finely chopped

1 garlic clove, minced

1 tablespoon chili powder

1 teaspoon ground coriander

1 can (14.5 ounces) crushed tomatoes

3 tablespoons pure maple syrup

2 tablespoons Worcestershire sauce

1 tablespoon tomato paste

2 dried bay leaves

2 thyme sprigs

Buns, for serving

1. Melt butter in a 6- to 8-quart stovetop pressure cooker over medium-high heat, or in an electric pressure cooker set to sauté. Add beef, pork, and veal, 1½ teaspoons salt, and ½ teaspoon pepper, and cook, breaking up with a wooden spoon, until meat is browned, about 6 minutes. Add onion, bell pepper, celery, and garlic, and cook, stirring occasionally, until onion is translucent, about 4 minutes. Add chili powder and coriander, and cook, stirring, until fragrant, about 30 seconds. Stir in tomatoes, maple syrup, Worcestershire, tomato paste, bay leaves, and thyme.

2. **STOVETOP:** Secure lid. Bring to high pressure over medium-high heat; reduce heat to maintain pressure and cook for 5 minutes. Remove from heat, quickly release pressure, then remove lid.

   ELECTRIC: Secure lid. Manually set cooker to 5 minutes and let it come to pressure. Once time is complete, turn off, quickly release pressure, then remove lid.

3. Discard bay leaves and thyme sprigs. Divide meat among buns and serve.

Ask your butcher for a combination of beef, pork, and veal, commonly referred to as **MEATLOAF MIX.**

LAMB SHANKS WITH PRUNES AND APRICOTS

This Moroccan stew is typically braised slowly in a tagine, a clay or ceramic pot whose shallow base and distinctive conical top allow steam to rise and then condense. Here, steam is also at work, but the process is intensified to tenderize the lamb and fruit and concentrate the fragrant spices. Serve this dish with basmati rice, couscous, or flatbread.

—————————————————— SERVES 3 TO 4 ——————————————————

4 garlic cloves

2 teaspoons ground cumin

½ teaspoon crumbled saffron threads

½ teaspoon ground cinnamon

Coarse salt and freshly ground pepper

3 large lamb shanks (about 3 pounds)

4 tablespoons unsalted butter

4 medium onions, halved lengthwise and thinly sliced crosswise

1 teaspoon cumin seeds

1 teaspoon aniseeds

1 (3-inch) cinnamon stick

2 cups water

1 cup pitted prunes or dried apricots or a mixture

Flatbread, basmati rice, or steamed couscous, for serving

1. With a mortar and pestle, grind garlic, cumin, saffron, cinnamon, 1 teaspoon salt, and ½ teaspoon pepper to a paste. Rub mixture all over lamb and let stand at room temperature for 1 hour, or refrigerate, covered, up to 8 hours.

2. Melt butter in a 6- to 8-quart stovetop pressure cooker over medium heat, or in an electric pressure cooker set to sauté. Cook onions, stirring occasionally, until softened, about 8 minutes. Add cumin seeds, aniseeds, cinnamon stick, and 1 teaspoon salt, and cook, stirring, 1 minute. Add the water and dried fruit. Arrange lamb shanks on top.

3. **STOVETOP:** Secure lid. Bring to high pressure over medium-high heat; reduce heat to maintain pressure and cook for 30 minutes. Remove from heat, quickly release pressure, then remove lid.

   ELECTRIC: Secure lid. Manually set cooker to 30 minutes and let it come to pressure. Once time is complete, turn off, quickly release pressure, then remove lid.

4. Discard cinnamon stick. Serve lamb with flatbread.

LAMB AND ROOT-VEGETABLE SOUP

Traditionally called Scotch broth, this soup, with lamb shanks as its mainstay, is heartier than its name implies. We love turnips, but you can swap in rutabaga, parsnips, or potatoes, if you like; just keep the pieces the same size so they cook evenly.

────────────────── **SERVES 6** ──────────────────

1 tablespoon extra-virgin olive oil

2 large lamb shanks (about 2 pounds)

Coarse salt and freshly ground pepper

1 large onion, finely chopped

3 garlic cloves, smashed

3 medium carrots, finely chopped

1 turnip, finely chopped

1 celery stalk, finely chopped

½ head green cabbage, cored and cut into 1-inch pieces

1 quart Chicken Stock, homemade (page 24) or store-bought

1 quart water

½ cup pearl barley

¼ cup Worcestershire sauce

4 whole cloves

2 dried bay leaves

Chopped fresh flat-leaf parsley (optional)

1. Heat oil in a 6- to 8-quart stovetop pressure cooker over high, or in an electric pressure cooker set to sauté. Pat lamb dry and season with ¾ teaspoon salt and ½ teaspoon pepper. Cook lamb until browned on all sides, about 10 minutes; transfer lamb to a plate. Cook onion and garlic, stirring, until softened and golden, about 6 minutes. Stir in carrots, turnip, celery, cabbage, stock, the water, barley, Worcestershire, cloves, bay leaves, and 1 teaspoon salt. Return lamb to pressure cooker along with any accumulated juices.

2. **STOVETOP:** Secure lid. Bring to high pressure over medium-high heat; reduce heat to maintain pressure and cook for 45 minutes. Remove from heat, quickly release pressure (loosely cover vent with a clean kitchen towel), then remove lid.

    ELECTRIC: Secure lid. Manually set cooker to 45 minutes and let it come to pressure. Once time is complete, turn off, quickly release pressure (loosely cover vent with a clean kitchen towel), then remove lid.

3. Let lamb stand in cooking liquid for 10 minutes. Transfer lamb to a cutting board and pull meat from bones. Using two forks, shred meat. Return lamb to pressure cooker, and season with salt and pepper. (Discard bay leaves.) Serve soup in bowls, topped with parsley, if desired.

LAMB AND POTATO CURRY

Curries are the perfect dishes for the pressure cooker, as the intense spices are quickly absorbed by the meat and potatoes. Serve this lamb shoulder curry with an array of condiments—chutneys, pickles, whole-milk yogurt—and some toasted Indian naan or pappadams.

SERVES 6 TO 8

---

3 tablespoons vegetable oil

2 medium onions, diced

3 tablespoons grated peeled fresh ginger

6 garlic cloves, minced

Coarse salt

1 (3-inch) cinnamon stick

2¼ teaspoons cumin seeds

1½ teaspoons coriander seeds, crushed

¾ teaspoon ground turmeric

2 cardamom pods, crushed

2 teaspoons tomato paste

2½ pounds boneless lamb shoulder, cut into 1-inch pieces

12 ounces baby fingerling potatoes

2 cups Chicken Stock, homemade (page 24) or store-bought

1 bunch spinach, trimmed (about 4 cups packed leaves)

Mint sprigs, for serving

Thinly sliced cucumbers, for serving

1. Heat oil in a 6- to 8-quart stovetop pressure cooker over medium-high, or in an electric pressure cooker set to sauté. Add onions, ginger, garlic, and 1 teaspoon salt. Cook, stirring occasionally, until onions are translucent, about 3 minutes. Add cinnamon stick, cumin and coriander seeds, turmeric, and cardamom. Cook, stirring, until spices are fragrant, about 30 seconds. Add tomato paste and cook, stirring to combine, 15 seconds more. Add lamb, potatoes, and stock; season with salt.

2. **STOVETOP:** Secure lid. Bring to high pressure over medium-high heat; reduce heat to maintain pressure and cook for 24 minutes. Remove from heat and let pressure decrease naturally for 10 minutes. Release remaining pressure, if necessary, then remove lid.

   ELECTRIC: Secure lid. Manually set cooker to 29 minutes and let it come to pressure. Once time is complete, turn off and let pressure decrease naturally for 10 minutes. Release remaining pressure, if necessary, then remove lid.

3. Stir in spinach. Season with salt. Top with mint and cucumber slices, and serve.

SALMON CHOWDER

Seafood cooks so quickly on the stovetop that you might question why you would even bother to use a pressure cooker. But the key here is using the high heat and intensity of the machine to build the flavor base, and then adding the fish at the very end, once the vegetables have cooked and the pressure has been released. We use a combination of bottled clam juice and water, but you can substitute a quart of home-made stock if you have it, or a high-quality stock from the fish market.

SERVES 8

- 4 slices bacon, cut crosswise into ¼-inch pieces
- 1 tablespoon unsalted butter
- 1 medium onion, finely chopped
- 1 cup dry white wine
- 1 pound Yukon Gold potatoes, peeled and cut into ½-inch cubes
- 2 cups bottled clam juice
- 2 cups water
- 1 cup heavy cream
  Coarse salt and freshly ground pepper
- 1 pound skinless salmon fillet, cut into 1-inch pieces
- ¼ cup snipped fresh chives or finely chopped fresh dill, for garnish

1. Heat a 6- to 8-quart stovetop pressure cooker over medium, or set an electric pressure cooker to sauté. Cook bacon, stirring occasionally, until browned but not crisp, about 5 minutes. Add butter and onion, and cook, stirring, until onion is softened, about 6 minutes. Add wine and boil until most of liquid is evaporated, about 5 minutes. Add potatoes, clam juice, the water, cream, and 1 teaspoon each salt and pepper.

2. **STOVETOP:** Secure lid. Bring to high pressure over medium-high heat; reduce heat to maintain pressure and cook for 5 minutes. Remove from heat, quickly release pressure, then remove lid. Return cooker to medium heat.

   ELECTRIC: Secure lid. Manually set cooker to 5 minutes and let it come to pressure. Once time is complete, turn off, quickly release pressure, then remove lid. Set cooker to sauté.

3. Season salmon with ½ teaspoon salt, then add to chowder. Cook until salmon is opaque and just cooked through, about 3 minutes. Season with salt and pepper, top with chives, and serve immediately.

SHELLFISH AND SAUSAGE STEW

Mixed seafood stews can be prepared in many, many ways—think bouillabaisse, cioppino, and all kinds of fish and shellfish chowders; it all depends on the day's catch. We found that heartier shellfish such as lobster and clams stood up to the pressure cooker's intense heat better than more delicate varieties, which cook quickly and may get rubbery. All you need on the side is some grilled bread, preferably brushed with oil and rubbed with garlic.

SERVES 6 TO 8

¼ cup extra-virgin olive oil

8 ounces smoked sausage, such as kielbasa, sliced into ¼-inch rounds

1 medium onion, chopped

3 garlic cloves, smashed

½ cup dry white or rosé wine

1 can (28 ounces) whole tomatoes

2 cups clam juice

2 pounds littleneck clams, scrubbed well

1 (1-pound) live lobster (optional), rubber bands removed from claws

8 ounces escarole

1 dried bay leaf

½ teaspoon red-pepper flakes

2 oregano or marjoram sprigs

Coarse salt and freshly ground black pepper

½ cup chopped fresh flat-leaf parsley, for garnish

1. Heat oil in a 6- to 8-quart stovetop pressure cooker over medium-high, or in an electric pressure cooker set to sauté. Add sausage, onion, and garlic, and cook, stirring occasionally, until onion is golden, about 6 minutes. Add wine and tomatoes (with their juices), breaking up tomatoes with a wooden spoon. Add clam juice, clams, lobster (if desired), escarole, bay leaf, red-pepper flakes, and oregano.

2. **STOVETOP:** Secure lid. Bring to high pressure over medium-high heat; reduce heat to maintain pressure and cook for 3 minutes. Remove from heat, quickly release pressure, then remove lid.

   ELECTRIC: Secure lid. Manually set cooker to 3 minutes and let it come to pressure. Once time is complete, turn off, quickly release pressure, then remove lid.

3. Transfer lobster to a plate. When cool enough to handle, snip tips off claws and let liquid drain out. Pull claws from bodies, completely separating. Twist tail from joint where it meets body. Use kitchen shears to slice down center of tail. Open sides of tail and use your fingers to pull out meat. Separate knuckles from claws. Crack knuckles open and remove meat with a small fork. Grasp "thumbs" from claws, and bend back to snap off. Place claws on their sides on a work surface. Holding with one hand, and using back of a chef's knife, whack several times to crack shells without cutting into meat. Twist to open and then pull out the meat with your fingers. Return meat to pressure cooker. (Discard bay leaf and oregano.)

4. Season stew with salt and black pepper, top with chopped parsley, and serve.

SHRIMP BISQUE

Bisque is a somewhat old-fashioned dish that deserves a comeback. Customarily, the shells of the shrimp are puréed into the broth to thicken and flavor the soup. In the pressure cooker, they are reserved to create a stock that gives the creamy soup a more intense taste of the sea. Paprika contributes to its pale pink hue. Serve the bisque as a first course at a dinner party, or as a main course with a toasted baguette and a crisp green salad.

——————————————— SERVES 4 ———————————————

1 pound medium shrimp (26 to 30 count), peeled, deveined, and halved lengthwise (reserving shells)

Coarse salt and freshly ground pepper

2 tablespoons cornstarch

3¼ cups water

1 cup dry white wine

¼ cup finely chopped onion

¼ cup finely chopped celery

¼ cup finely chopped carrot

1 teaspoon paprika

1 cup heavy cream

2 tablespoons chopped fresh dill

1 tablespoon unsalted butter

Watercress or fresh dill, for garnish

Toasted baguette, for serving

1. Toss shrimp with ½ teaspoon salt in a small bowl. In another small bowl, stir cornstarch and ¼ cup water until smooth.

2. In a 6- to 8-quart pressure cooker, combine shrimp shells, remaining 3 cups water, the wine, onion, celery, carrot, ½ teaspoon salt, and ¼ teaspoon pepper.

3. **STOVETOP:** Secure lid. Bring to high pressure over medium-high heat; reduce heat to maintain pressure and cook for 8 minutes. Remove from heat, quickly release pressure, then remove lid.

   ELECTRIC: Secure lid. Manually set cooker to 10 minutes and let it come to pressure. Once time is complete, turn off, quickly release pressure, then remove lid.

4. Strain stock through a medium-mesh sieve set over a large bowl, pressing on solids (discard solids). Return stock to cooker, add paprika and cream, and bring to a boil in a stovetop cooker over medium heat or in an electric cooker set to sauté. Whisk cornstarch-water mixture into soup to thicken slightly, 1 to 2 minutes. Add shrimp and cook, stirring, until just cooked through, about 3 minutes.

5. Season with salt and pepper, then stir in dill and butter. Top with watercress and serve immediately with a toasted baguette.

SAFFRON RISOTTO WITH CLAMS

The proper risotto consistency is easily achieved using the pressure cooker, without the need to ladle in warm stock and stir (and stir) until it is absorbed. On the next few pages, you have three opportunities to master risotto, starting with the Milanese version, which gets its golden color from saffron. We added clams, steaming them separately to avoid overcooking and to use their briny liquid as a stock for the dish.

SERVES 8

3 pounds littleneck or Manila clams, scrubbed well

2 cups water

6 tablespoons unsalted butter

½ cup minced shallots

2 large garlic cloves, minced

½ teaspoon crumbled saffron threads

3 cups Arborio rice

1 cup dry white wine

¼ cup coarsely chopped fresh flat-leaf parsley or dill, plus sprigs for garnish

Coarse salt and freshly ground pepper

1. Combine clams and the water in a medium pot. Cover, bring to a boil, and cook until clams begin to open, about 4 minutes. Uncover and continue to cook, stirring occasionally, until all clams open (discard any unopened clams); transfer clams to a bowl. Pour cooking liquid through a fine-mesh sieve set over a large heatproof bowl; add enough water to make 7 cups. Once cool, remove clams from their shells; transfer to a bowl.

2. Melt butter in a 6- to 8-quart stovetop pressure cooker over medium heat, or in an electric pressure cooker set to sauté. Add shallots, garlic, and saffron, and cook, stirring, until softened, about 3 minutes. Add rice and stir to coat, about 1 minute. Add wine and cook, stirring, until almost absorbed, about 1 minute. Add clam cooking liquid.

3. **STOVETOP:** Secure lid. Bring to high pressure over medium-high heat; reduce heat to maintain pressure and cook 5 minutes for al dente, 6 minutes for fully cooked rice. Remove from heat, quickly release pressure (loosely cover vent with a clean kitchen towel), then remove lid.

   ELECTRIC: Secure lid. Manually set cooker to 6 minutes for al dente, 7 minutes for fully cooked rice, and let it come to pressure. Once time is complete, turn off, quickly release pressure (loosely cover vent with a clean kitchen towel), then remove lid.

4. Stir in reserved clams and the chopped parsley, and season with salt and pepper. Top with parsley sprigs and serve.

If the **RISOTTO** is too soupy, add a minute or two to the cooking time; if it is too dry, add more liquid.

CORN RISOTTO WITH BASIL AND TOMATOES

Save this risotto for the summertime, to make the most of the season's peak ingredients. To create a broth that infuses the risotto with incomparable corn flavor, first remove the corn kernels from the cobs, then add the cobs to the pressure cooker while the rice cooks. Fresh basil, another highlight of summer, provides the perfect finishing touch.

SERVES 6 TO 8

- 2 tablespoons unsalted butter
- 1 medium onion, finely chopped
- 1 garlic clove, smashed

  Coarse salt and freshly ground pepper
- 1½ cups Arborio rice
- ½ cup dry white wine
- 1 quart water
- 3 ears corn, kernels removed (about 2¼ cups) and cobs reserved
- 1 pint cherry tomatoes, halved or quartered if large
- ½ cup finely grated Parmigiano-Reggiano cheese (2 ounces), plus shaved for garnish

  Fresh basil, for garnish

1. Melt butter in a 6- to 8-quart stovetop pressure cooker over medium-high heat, or in an electric pressure cooker set to sauté. Add onion, garlic, and 1 teaspoon salt, and cook, stirring occasionally, until golden and softened, about 6 minutes. Add rice and stir to coat, about 1 minute. Add wine and cook, stirring, until almost absorbed, about 1 minute. Add the water and reserved corncobs.

2. **STOVETOP:** Secure lid. Bring to high pressure over medium-high heat; reduce heat to maintain pressure and cook 5 minutes for al dente, 6 minutes for fully cooked rice. Remove from heat, quickly release pressure (loosely cover vent with a clean kitchen towel), then remove lid.

   ELECTRIC: Secure lid. Manually set cooker to 6 minutes for al dente, 7 minutes for fully cooked rice, and let it come to pressure. Once time is complete, turn off, quickly release pressure (loosely cover vent with a clean kitchen towel), then remove lid.

3. Remove corncobs from pressure cooker and discard. Stir in corn kernels, tomatoes, and grated cheese; season with salt and pepper. Top with shaved cheese and basil, and serve immediately.

MUSHROOM RISOTTO

A fresh-mushroom risotto already has a healthy umami factor, but adding even a small amount of dried porcini or oyster mushrooms gives it a huge boost. Dried shiitakes, which are equally meaty and have a slightly less pronounced taste, are another delicious option. There's no need to soak the dried mushrooms, as the pressure cooker takes care of hydrating them and allowing them to infuse the rice with their earthy flavor.

SERVES 6 TO 8

- 2 tablespoons extra-virgin olive oil
- 1 medium onion, finely chopped
- 2 garlic cloves, smashed

  Coarse salt and freshly ground pepper
- 1 pound fresh mushrooms, such as porcini or oyster, torn if large
- 1½ cups Arborio rice
- ½ cup dry white wine
- 1 quart water
- ½ ounce dried mushrooms, such as porcini or oyster
- ½ cup finely grated Parmigiano-Reggiano cheese (2 ounces)

  Snipped fresh chives, for garnish

1. Heat oil in a 6- to 8-quart stovetop pressure cooker over medium, or in an electric pressure cooker set to sauté. Add onion, garlic, and 1 teaspoon salt, and cook, stirring occasionally, until golden and softened, about 6 minutes. Stir in fresh mushrooms and cook until their liquid is released, 3 to 6 minutes. Add rice and stir to coat, about 1 minute. Add wine and cook, stirring, until almost absorbed, about 1 minute. Add the water and dried mushrooms.

2. **STOVETOP:** Secure lid. Bring to high pressure over medium-high heat; reduce heat to maintain pressure and cook 5 minutes for al dente, 6 minutes for fully cooked rice. Remove from heat, quickly release pressure (loosely cover vent with a clean kitchen towel), then remove lid.

   ELECTRIC: Secure lid. Manually set cooker to 6 minutes for al dente, 7 minutes for fully cooked rice, and let it come to pressure. Once time is complete, turn off, quickly release pressure (loosely cover vent with a clean kitchen towel), then remove lid.

3. Stir in cheese, and season with salt and pepper. Top with chives and serve immediately.

DRIED MUSHROOMS usually need to be rehydrated by soaking in water, but you can skip this step in the pressure cooker. If you're worried about grit, simply soak the mushrooms for 30 minutes, strain to remove grit, and rinse. Replace some of the water with mushroom stock to retain every ounce of umami flavor.

THAI RED CURRY WITH BUTTERNUT SQUASH

Cooked in the pressure cooker in under an hour, winter squash takes on a velvety texture, which blends well with the ingredients of a Thai curry. You can substitute just about any winter squash that looks good at the market—such as acorn, kabocha, or pumpkin. The noodles don't get added until the end, after the pressure is vented; it takes a quick five minutes to reach tender perfection.

━━━━━━━━━━━━━━━━ **SERVES 4 TO 6** ━━━━━━━━━━━━━━━━

- 3 tablespoons extra-virgin olive oil
- 2 large shallots, thinly sliced
- 4 garlic cloves, smashed
- 4 ounces shiitake mushrooms, stemmed and sliced
- 1½ tablespoons Thai red curry paste
- 2 tablespoons fish sauce, such as *nuoc nam* or *nam pla*
- 1 butternut squash (3 pounds), peeled, seeded, and cut into 2-inch pieces
- 1 can (14 ounces) unsweetened coconut milk
- 1½ cups water

  Coarse salt and freshly ground pepper
- 2 ounces dried rice stick noodles, preferably brown
- 2 tablespoons fresh lime juice

  Roasted peanuts and fresh cilantro, for serving

1. Heat oil in a 6- to 8-quart stovetop pressure cooker over medium-high, or in an electric pressure cooker set to sauté. Add shallots, garlic, and mushrooms, and cook, stirring, until shallots are golden, 6 to 8 minutes. Add curry paste and fish sauce, and cook, stirring, until fragrant, about 1 minute. Add squash, coconut milk, the water, and ½ teaspoon each salt and pepper.

2. **STOVETOP:** Secure lid. Bring to high pressure over medium-high heat; reduce heat to maintain pressure and cook for 12 minutes. Remove from heat, quickly release pressure, then remove lid.

   ELECTRIC: Secure lid. Manually set cooker to 15 minutes and let it come to pressure. Once time is complete, turn off, quickly release pressure, then remove lid.

3. Stir in rice noodles and let stand until tender, about 5 minutes. Add lime juice and stir to combine. Transfer curry to bowls, and top with peanuts and cilantro before serving.

RED CURRY PASTE usually combines dried red chiles with garlic, lemongrass, shallots, cilantro, kaffir lime leaves, and galangal, along with shrimp or fish paste.

BRAISED VEGETABLES WITH COUSCOUS

FOR THE VEGETABLES

- 4 tablespoons unsalted butter
- Pinch saffron threads
- 1 or 2 cups water
- 2 (3-inch) cinnamon sticks
- Coarse salt and freshly ground pepper
- 1 small butternut squash, peeled and seeded
- 2 small onions, halved
- 2 medium turnips, peeled
- 2 medium summer squash, 1 green and 1 yellow
- ½ head cauliflower
- 3 medium carrots
- 1 cup cooked chickpeas (pages 30–31), drained
- 1 to 2 tablespoons harissa

FOR THE COUSCOUS

- 2 cups couscous
- 2¼ cups water
- 2 tablespoons unsalted butter
- Pinch saffron threads, crumbled
- 1 (3-inch) cinnamon stick
- Coarse salt

This version of couscous, a signature of Moroccan cooking, features an array of colorful vegetables fragrant with saffron and cinnamon and a harissa-spiked broth. It's best served in the traditional way—on a large platter that allows everyone to help themselves.

──────────── SERVES 8 ────────────

1. **MAKE THE VEGETABLES:** Melt butter with saffron in a 6- to 8-quart stovetop pressure cooker over medium heat, or in an electric pressure cooker set to sauté. Add water (2 cups for stovetop; 1 cup for electric), cinnamon sticks, and 2 teaspoons each salt and pepper. Cut butternut squash, onions, turnips, and summer squash into 1-inch pieces. Cut cauliflower into 2-inch florets. Cut carrots into ½-inch slices. Add vegetables and chickpeas to cooker.

2. **STOVETOP:** Secure lid. Bring to high pressure over medium-high heat; reduce heat to maintain pressure and cook for 2 minutes. Remove from heat, quickly release pressure, then remove lid.

   ELECTRIC: Secure lid. Manually set cooker to 3 minutes and let it come to pressure. Once time is complete, turn off, quickly release pressure, then remove lid.

3. **MAKE THE COUSCOUS:** Place couscous in a large heatproof bowl. In a small pot, bring water to a boil with butter, saffron, cinnamon stick, and 1 teaspoon salt, stirring until butter is melted. Pour mixture over couscous. Tightly cover bowl with a lid, and let stand until liquid is absorbed and couscous is tender, about 5 minutes. Fluff couscous with a fork (discard cinnamon).

4. Drain liquid from vegetables into a small bowl and whisk in harissa to taste. Transfer couscous to a large platter, top with vegetables, and drizzle with harissa broth. Serve immediately.

TEMPEH WITH TERIYAKI GREENS AND CILANTRO YOGURT

5 tablespoons extra-virgin olive oil

2 packages (8 ounces each) plain tempeh, cut into 8 pieces total

1 large shallot, thinly sliced

2 garlic cloves, finely chopped

1 tablespoon minced peeled fresh ginger

4 ounces shiitake mushrooms, stemmed and thinly sliced

¾ or 1¼ cups water

¼ cup soy sauce

3 tablespoons sugar

2 tablespoons apple cider vinegar

Coarse salt and freshly ground pepper

1 pound spinach or Swiss chard, trimmed and coarsely chopped, including stems

1 bunch fresh cilantro

1 cup Greek whole-milk yogurt

Protein-packed tofu and tempeh take especially kindly to the pressure cooker. When these soy-based ingredients are combined with vegetables and spices, they acquire a deliciously complex flavor, as they absorb the essence of everything that accompanies them in the pot. Here, the tempeh is browned first, then paired with aromatics and hardy greens, and finished with a refreshing cilantro yogurt.

— SERVES 4 —

1. Heat 2 tablespoons oil in a 6- to 8-quart stovetop pressure cooker over medium-high, or in an electric pressure cooker set to sauté. Add half the tempeh and cook, turning once, until golden brown, about 5 minutes; transfer to a plate. Repeat with 2 tablespoons oil and remaining tempeh; transfer to plate.

2. Add remaining tablespoon oil, the shallot, garlic, ginger, and mushrooms, and cook, stirring, until shallots are golden, 6 to 8 minutes. Add water (1¼ cups for stovetop; ¾ cup for electric), soy sauce, sugar, vinegar, and ½ teaspoon each salt and pepper. Return tempeh to cooker.

3. **STOVETOP:** Secure lid. Bring to high pressure over medium-high heat; reduce heat to maintain pressure and cook for 10 minutes. Remove from heat, quickly release pressure, then remove lid. Add spinach. Secure lid and bring to high pressure over medium-high heat, then quickly release pressure and remove lid.

   ELECTRIC: Secure lid. Manually set cooker to 12 minutes and let it come to pressure. Once time is complete, turn off, quickly release pressure, then remove lid. Add spinach. Secure lid. Manually set pressure to 1 minute and let it come to pressure. Once time is complete, turn off, quickly release pressure, then remove lid.

4. Meanwhile, purée cilantro, yogurt, and ½ teaspoon salt in a blender or food processor until smooth. Serve tempeh and spinach with cilantro yogurt.

RAJAS TAMALES

For traditionally steamed foods like tamales, the pressure cooker really comes in handy. We absolutely love the way it produces incredibly tender, fluffy tamales in about 15 minutes. Strips of roasted poblano chiles, known as *rajas,* add a rich smokiness to many Mexican dishes—whether folded into tacos and tamales or served as a side with grilled meat. You can find dried corn husks and masa harina in the Latin aisle of many large grocery stores and specialty markets.

MAKES ABOUT 20 TAMALES

---

25 dried corn husks

2 large poblano chiles

2 sticks (1 cup) unsalted butter, softened

3 cups masa harina for tamales

Coarse salt

2 cups warm water, plus 3 cups for pressure cooker

2 cups shredded Monterey Jack cheese (8 ounces)

Fresh cilantro, for serving

Salsa, for serving

1. Place corn husks in a large bowl, cover with cold water, and weigh down with a plate to keep husks submerged. Soak until softened and pliable, about 30 minutes.

2. Heat broiler with rack 4 inches from heating element. Cut poblanos in half lengthwise and remove ribs and seeds. Place cut side down on a baking sheet, and broil, turning often, until charred on all sides, about 8 minutes. Transfer to a bowl, cover with plastic wrap, and let stand for 15 minutes. When cool enough to handle, rub with a paper towel to remove skins, being careful not to tear flesh. Cut into thin strips.

3. With a mixer, beat butter until light and creamy, about 2 minutes. With your hands, mix masa harina, 1 teaspoon salt, and the warm water until it forms a dough. Add masa mixture to butter and continue to beat until light and fluffy, about 2 minutes.

4. Remove husks from water, letting excess drip off. Working in batches, lay husks on a work surface, long sides closest to you. Tear two to three husks into ¼-inch strips; reserve for tying. Spread about ¼ cup dough thinly on center of each husk into about a 3-by-4-inch rectangle. Place a few poblano strips and a rounded tablespoon cheese in the center of dough. Bring together two long sides, to encase dough. Fold in two shorter sides. Use a strip of husk to tie tamale loosely closed.

recipe continues

5. Place a 1-inch rack in 6- to 8-quart pressure cooker and fill with 3 cups water. Place the steamer insert on rack. Place tamales standing upright in steamer insert.

   STOVETOP: Secure lid. Bring to high pressure over medium-high heat; reduce heat to maintain pressure and cook for 15 minutes. Remove from heat, quickly release pressure, then remove lid. Let cool slightly.

   ELECTRIC: Secure lid. Manually set cooker to 15 minutes and let it come to pressure. Once time is complete, turn off, quickly release pressure, then remove lid. Let cool slightly.

6. Serve with cilantro and salsa.

Try these variations on the basic masa dough by adding a few fresh ingredients at the end of Step 3. For **HERB TAMALES**, stir 1½ cups mixed chopped fresh herbs, such as basil, chives, tarragon, cilantro, and parsley, and ½ cup chopped scallions into dough and enclose in corn husks. To make **CORN AND BASIL TAMALES**, stir 1½ cups steamed fresh or thawed frozen corn kernels, ½ cup sliced scallions, and ¼ cup chopped basil into dough and enclose in corn husks. Serve either variation with salsa and scallions.

MEXICAN TORTILLA SOUP

Ancho, pasilla, and chipotle chiles turn up the heat in this Mexican chicken soup. Tucking chicken wings into a cheesecloth bundle and cooking them alongside the other ingredients produces a full-bodied broth with intense chicken flavor.

SERVES 8

1 large dried ancho chile, stemmed and seeded

1 large dried pasilla chile, stemmed and seeded

1 pound chicken wings

Coarse salt

1 medium onion, chopped

3 garlic cloves, smashed

1 can (14.5 ounces) crushed tomatoes

½ pound tomatillos, husked, rinsed, and quartered

½ cup chopped fresh cilantro, plus more for garnish

1 chipotle chile in adobo, plus 1 tablespoon adobo sauce

6 cups water

1 pound bone-in, skin-on chicken thighs

Vegetable oil, for frying

4 (7-inch) corn tortillas, cut into thin strips, for serving

Chopped avocados, diced queso fresco, lime wedges, for serving (optional)

1. Heat a flat griddle or dry skillet over medium-low. Add ancho and pasilla chiles; toast, pressing and turning with tongs, until fragrant, about 1 minute.

2. Place chicken on a 16-inch square of cheesecloth and season with salt; tie opposite corners of cloth together to form a bundle.

3. Purée toasted chiles, onion, garlic, tomatoes, tomatillos, cilantro, chipotle and adobo sauce, and 2 cups water in a blender until smooth. Place chile mixture, chicken wing bundle, chicken thighs, remaining 1 quart water, and 2 teaspoons salt in a 6- to 8-quart pressure cooker.

4. **STOVETOP:** Secure lid. Bring to high pressure over medium-high heat; reduce heat to maintain pressure and cook for 16 minutes. Remove from heat, quickly release pressure, then remove lid. Let chicken stand in liquid for 10 minutes.

   ELECTRIC: Secure lid. Manually set cooker to 20 minutes and let it come to pressure. Once time is complete, turn off, quickly release pressure, then remove lid. Let chicken stand in liquid for 10 minutes.

5. Meanwhile, in a large straight-sided skillet, pour oil to a depth of 2½ inches. Add tortilla strips and cook until golden, about 2 minutes. With a slotted spoon, transfer tortilla strips to a paper-towel–lined plate. Sprinkle lightly with salt.

6. Remove wing bundle and press to extract any liquid. Skim any fat from surface, and season with salt.

7. Divide chicken thighs among bowls. Add soup, and top with tortilla strips and cilantro. Serve with avocado, queso fresco, and lime wedges, if desired.

MEXICAN TORTILLA SOUP

GARLIC-AND-BREAD SOUP

VIETNAMESE-STYLE CHICKEN SOUP

GARLIC-AND-BREAD SOUP

This classic Spanish soup known as *sopa de ajo* works especially well in the pressure cooker because the machine magically mellows the garlic. Bread and eggs are added at the end to transform this into an incredibly comforting dish.

SERVES 6

1½ pounds chicken wings

Coarse salt and freshly ground pepper

¼ cup extra-virgin olive oil

10 garlic cloves, thinly sliced

1½ teaspoons sweet smoked paprika

6 cups water

6 ounces good-quality white country bread (about 5 slices), toasted and torn into pieces

6 large eggs

1. Place chicken wings on a 16-inch square of cheesecloth and season with salt, then tie opposite corners of cloth together to form a bundle.

2. Heat oil in a 6- to 8-quart stovetop pressure cooker over medium-high, or in an electric pressure cooker set to sauté. Add garlic and cook, stirring, until golden, about 2 minutes. Add paprika and cook, stirring, until fragrant, about 30 seconds. Stir in the water, chicken wing bundle, 2 teaspoons salt, and ½ teaspoon pepper.

3. **STOVETOP:** Secure lid. Bring to high pressure over medium-high heat; reduce heat to maintain pressure and cook for 20 minutes. Remove from heat, quickly release pressure, then remove lid.

   ELECTRIC: Secure lid. Manually set cooker to 25 minutes and let it come to pressure. Once time is complete, turn off, quickly release pressure, then remove lid.

4. Remove chicken wing bundle (see tip below). Bring soup to a gentle simmer over medium heat or using the sauté function. Season soup with salt and stir in bread. Crack one egg into a ramekin, then gently slide egg into soup. Repeat with remaining eggs. Cook until whites are set and yolks are still runny, 3 to 4 minutes. Serve immediately.

Once you remove the **CHICKEN WINGS** from the soups on these pages and on page 191, you can fry them up: Let cool, pat dry, and season with salt and pepper. In a skillet, heat an inch of oil over medium-high. Drop wings into skillet and cook until golden and crisp, about 10 minutes.

VIETNAMESE-STYLE CHICKEN SOUP

Fresh herbs are essential to Vietnamese cooking, and this soup is fragrant with ginger, cilantro, lemongrass, and mint. Mushrooms and fish sauce add a healthy dose of umami to the chicken. However, unlike the classic Vietnamese pho, noodles are not included, and we added bacon.

SERVES 6 TO 8

1½ **pounds chicken wings**

4 **ounces bacon (about 4 slices), finely chopped**

¼ **cup finely chopped fresh lemongrass (about 4 stalks, bottom 3 inches only)**

¼ **cup finely chopped fresh cilantro**

3 **tablespoons minced peeled fresh ginger**

3 **garlic cloves, smashed**

¼ **cup fish sauce, such as** *nuoc nam* **or** *nam pla*

3 **quarts water**

2 **large bone-in, skin-on chicken thighs**

8 **ounces cremini mushrooms, sliced**

2 **teaspoons coarse salt**

⅓ **cup fresh lime juice, plus lime wedges, for serving**

Fresh mint leaves and avocado slices, for garnish

1. Place chicken wings on a 16-inch square of cheesecloth; tie opposite corners of cloth together to form a bundle.

2. Heat a 6- to 8-quart stovetop pressure cooker over medium-high, or set an electric pressure cooker to sauté. Add bacon and cook until some fat is rendered, about 6 minutes. Add lemongrass, cilantro, ginger, and garlic, and cook, stirring occasionally, until golden and fragrant, about 3 minutes. Stir in fish sauce, scraping up any browned bits with a wooden spoon. Stir in the water, chicken wing bundle, chicken thighs, mushrooms, and salt.

3. **STOVETOP:** Secure lid. Bring to high pressure over medium-high heat; reduce heat to maintain pressure and cook for 20 minutes. Remove from heat, quickly release pressure, then remove lid.

   ELECTRIC: Secure lid. Manually set cooker to 25 minutes and let it come to pressure. Once time is complete, turn off, quickly release pressure, then remove lid.

4. Let chicken stand in liquid for 10 minutes. Remove chicken wing bundle. Skim any fat from surface of soup, if desired.

5. Transfer chicken thighs to a cutting board. Remove skin from chicken thighs and pull meat from bones. Using two forks, shred chicken into pieces (discard bones and skin). Return chicken to soup. Stir in lime juice, top with mint leaves and avocado, and serve with lime wedges.

THREE-BEAN RIBOLLITA

4 ounces bacon, cut into ½-inch pieces

1 onion, cut into ½-inch pieces

2 garlic cloves, minced

3 ounces dried cannellini beans (½ cup)

3 ounces dried Great Northern beans (½ cup)

3 ounces dried pinto beans (½ cup)

4 carrots, cut into ½-inch pieces

2 celery stalks, cut into ½-inch pieces

5½ cups Chicken Stock, homemade (page 24) or store-bought

3½ cups water

Coarse salt and freshly ground pepper

½ savoy cabbage (about 12 ounces), thinly sliced

2 teaspoons chopped fresh rosemary

6 slices day-old country-style bread, torn into small pieces

Finely grated Parmigiano-Reggiano, for serving

Extra-virgin olive oil, for serving (optional)

Ribollita means "reboiled" in Italian. In Tuscany, this hearty soup was invented by frugal cooks who wanted to use up leftovers, such as a pot of minestrone and yesterday's bread. Our ribollita uses day-old bread but we made the soup itself from scratch, and it is one soothing, satisfying meal.

—————————— SERVES 8 ——————————

1. Heat a 6- to 8-quart stovetop pressure cooker over medium-high, or set an electric pressure cooker to sauté. Add bacon and cook, stirring occasionally, until crisp, about 6 minutes. With a slotted spoon, transfer bacon to a paper-towel-lined plate. Add onion and garlic to pressure cooker, and cook until softened, 6 to 8 minutes. Add beans, carrots, celery, stock, and the water. Season with salt and pepper.

2. **STOVETOP:** Secure lid. Bring to high pressure over medium-high heat; reduce heat to maintain pressure and cook for 50 minutes. Remove from heat, quickly release pressure (loosely cover vent with a clean kitchen towel), then remove lid. Let stand 10 minutes. Bring to a simmer over medium heat.

   ELECTRIC: Secure lid. Manually set cooker to 30 minutes and let it come to pressure. Once time is complete, turn off, quickly release pressure (loosely cover vent with a clean kitchen towel), then remove lid. Let stand 10 minutes. Bring to a simmer using the sauté function.

3. Add cabbage and rosemary, and cook, stirring, until cabbage is tender, 5 to 10 minutes. Stir in bread and simmer until bread has softened and begins to break down, about 2 minutes. Stir in reserved bacon, and season with salt and pepper. Sprinkle with cheese and drizzle with oil, if desired, and serve immediately.

If you don't have **DAY-OLD BREAD,** spread slices or cubes of fresh country-style bread on a rimmed baking sheet and toast in a 300°F oven for about 15 minutes.

BLACK BEAN SOUP WITH RADISH AND EGG

1 pound dried black beans

2 or 2½ quarts water

1 smoked ham hock or shank (or substitute Ham Stock, page 25, for 1 quart of the water)

2 tablespoons extra-virgin olive oil

2 medium onions, coarsely chopped

1 medium carrot, coarsely chopped

1 small green bell pepper, ribs and seeds removed, coarsely chopped

1 medium parsnip, coarsely chopped

3 garlic cloves, coarsely chopped

1 teaspoon ground cumin

Coarse salt and freshly ground pepper

½ cup cream sherry

2 hard-cooked eggs, peeled and sliced, for garnish

2 radishes, sliced into matchsticks, for garnish

Cooking the beans with the aromatics from the start produces a full-bodied soup. A cured ham hock provides smoky depth; ham stock achieves that same flavor, if you have a batch frozen. For nutty warmth, we added sweet cream sherry, but you could also use dry sherry or Shaoxing.

———————— **SERVES 6 TO 8** ————————

1. In a 6- to 8-quart pressure cooker, combine beans, the water (2½ quarts for stovetop; 2 quarts for electric), ham hock, oil, onions, carrot, bell pepper, parsnip, garlic, cumin, and ½ teaspoon pepper.

2. **STOVETOP:** Secure lid. Bring to high pressure over medium-high heat; reduce heat to maintain pressure and cook for 25 minutes. Remove from heat, quickly release pressure (loosely cover vent with a clean kitchen towel), then remove lid.

   ELECTRIC: Secure lid. Manually set cooker to 30 minutes and let it come to pressure. Once time is complete, turn off, quickly release pressure (loosely cover vent with a clean kitchen towel), then remove lid.

3. Remove ham hock and reserve. Add sherry and 1 teaspoon salt, or to taste. Shred or coarsely chop meat from ham hock and return to soup. Serve soup topped with sliced egg and radish.

RED LENTIL AND GINGER DAL

Unlike brown or green lentils, red lentils cook quickly, breaking down to a creamy consistency. They are the foundation for many soups and stews (including the ubiquitous dal) in Indian and other Southeast Asian cuisines. This version features a generous amount of fresh ginger and is served with yogurt to counterbalance the heat of the soup. You can also finish the dish with lime pickle, an Indian condiment made with salted, fermented limes. It packs a bright, powerful punch, so if you've never tried it, start with a small amount and adjust to your liking.

SERVES 6

- 3 tablespoons extra-virgin olive oil
- 1 large onion, finely chopped
- 4 garlic cloves, minced
- 3 tablespoons minced peeled fresh ginger
- 1 teaspoon ground cumin
- ½ teaspoon curry powder
- 4 or 6 cups water, plus more as needed
- 2 plum tomatoes, finely chopped
- 2 cups red lentils, picked over and rinsed
- 1 bay leaf
- Coarse salt and freshly ground pepper
- Plain whole-milk yogurt, for serving
- Lime pickle, finely chopped, for serving (optional)

1. Heat oil in a 6- to 8-quart pressure cooker over medium-high, or in an electric pressure cooker set to sauté. Add onion, garlic, and ginger, and cook, stirring, until softened, about 6 minutes. Add cumin and curry powder, and cook, stirring to combine, 1 minute. Add water (6 cups for stovetop; 4 cups for electric), tomatoes, red lentils, bay leaf, 2 teaspoons salt, and 1 teaspoon pepper.

2. **STOVETOP:** Secure lid. Bring to high pressure over medium-high heat; reduce heat to maintain pressure and cook for 10 minutes. Remove from heat, quickly release pressure (loosely cover vent with a clean kitchen towel), then remove lid.

   ELECTRIC: Secure lid. Manually set cooker to 10 minutes and let it come to pressure. Once time is complete, turn off, quickly release pressure (loosely cover vent with a clean kitchen towel), then remove lid.

3. If stew is too thick, add up to 1 cup water, a few tablespoons at a time. (Discard bay leaf.) Season with salt and pepper. Serve with yogurt and lime pickle, if desired.

RAMEN WITH SHIITAKE MUSHROOMS

Of all the different stocks we made in the pressure cooker, ham stock was the most surprising—in a delightful way. It's hugely versatile, and we especially love it as the base for ramen. To begin building the soup, the garlic, ginger, diced ham, and shiitakes are sautéed together before the stock and water are added. For this recipe, fresh ramen noodles, which are more springy and chewy, are preferable to dried. Serve this comforting soup as is or topped with a soft-cooked egg and a drizzle of chili oil.

SERVES 6

3 tablespoons unsalted butter

7 ounces shiitake mushrooms, destemmed and thinly sliced

1 garlic clove, smashed

1 tablespoon minced peeled fresh ginger

1 quart Ham Stock, plus 4 ounces (¾ cup) cooked diced ham (page 25)

1 quart water

Coarse salt and freshly ground pepper

12 ounces fresh ramen noodles

4 ounces mustard greens, such as mizuna

Thinly sliced scallions, for garnish

Lime wedges, for serving (optional)

1. Melt butter in a 6- to 8-quart pressure cooker over medium-high heat, or in an electric pressure cooker set to sauté. Add mushrooms, garlic, and ginger, and cook, stirring occasionally, until golden, about 4 minutes. Add ham and cook, stirring, until browned, about 2 minutes. Add stock, the water, 1 teaspoon salt, and ½ teaspoon pepper.

2. **STOVETOP:** Secure lid. Bring to high pressure over medium-high heat; reduce heat to maintain pressure and cook for 1 minute. Remove from heat, quickly release pressure, then remove lid. Return cooker to medium-high heat.

   ELECTRIC: Secure lid. Manually set cooker to 1 minute and let it come to pressure. Once time is complete, turn off, quickly release pressure, then remove lid. Set cooker to sauté.

3. Bring broth to a boil. Add noodles and cook, stirring occasionally, until tender, 2 to 3 minutes.

4. Divide noodles among bowls. Ladle broth over noodles. Stir in greens and top with sliced scallions. Serve with lime wedges, if desired.

FRESH RAMEN NOODLES can be found in the refrigerated section of Asian grocers and large supermarkets.

MINESTRONE

There are countless versions of minestrone—some with beans, some with potatoes, some with pasta, some with all three. This one features potatoes, tomatoes, home-made vegetable stock, and fresh herbs. If you have a parmesan cheese rind in your refrigerator, do what many an Italian grandmother does and add it to the soup with the tomatoes. As the rind softens, it adds richness. You can finish with good-quality olive oil and a hefty pinch of red-pepper flakes. Grilled bread and a crisp green salad turn this dish into a meal.

--- **SERVES 6** ---

3 tablespoons unsalted butter

1 medium onion, finely chopped

2 garlic cloves, minced

Coarse salt and freshly ground pepper

2 medium carrots, finely chopped

1 large celery stalk, finely chopped

1 medium red bell pepper, ribs and seeds removed, finely chopped

1 large potato, finely chopped

1 quart Vegetable Stock, homemade (page 26) or store-bought

1 can (28 ounces) plum tomatoes

Shaved Parmigiano-Reggiano cheese and herb sprigs, such as oregano or basil, for serving

1. Melt butter in a 6- to 8-quart stovetop pressure cooker over medium-high heat, or in an electric pressure cooker set to sauté. Add onion, garlic, and 1 teaspoon salt. Cook, stirring occasionally, until golden, 6 to 8 minutes. Add carrots, celery, bell pepper, potato, stock, tomatoes (with their juices), and ½ teaspoon pepper.

2. **STOVETOP:** Secure lid. Bring to high pressure over medium-high heat; reduce heat to maintain pressure and cook for 10 minutes. Remove from heat, quickly release pressure, then remove lid.

   ELECTRIC: Secure lid. Manually set cooker to 10 minutes and let it come to pressure. Once time is complete, turn off, quickly release pressure, then remove lid.

3. Season with salt and pepper. Serve topped with shaved cheese and an herb sprig.

Always have supper at the ready by dividing a batch of minestrone into smaller portions and **FREEZING,** in resealable bags, for up to 3 months. Then simply thaw, reheat, and serve—topped with fresh herbs and cheese.

SPRING VEGETABLE SOUP

The appeal of this soup—in addition to its striking green color—is its versatility: You can use any combination of delicate herbs and green vegetables you wish. Blending the herbs and garlic into the cooked vegetable base adds brightness, providing a nice balance for the butter and cream. This is prepared as a warm soup, but for those days when cold soup would hit the spot, simply use olive oil in place of the butter so the fat remains a liquid.

SERVES 6

5 cups Vegetable Stock, homemade (page 26) or store-bought, or water

5 cups chopped mixed green vegetables (about 12 ounces), such as lettuce, sorrel, green beans, asparagus, peas, spinach, and scallion greens

1 large shallot, coarsely chopped

1 medium potato, cut into 1-inch pieces

1 medium tomato, quartered

1 cup mixed coarsely chopped fresh herbs, such as chives, chervil, parsley, dill, and basil

1 garlic clove

Coarse salt and freshly ground pepper

2 tablespoons unsalted butter

Heavy cream, at room temperature, for serving

1. Place stock, green vegetables, shallot, potato, and tomato in a 6- to 8-quart pressure cooker.

2. **STOVETOP:** Secure lid. Bring to high pressure over medium-high heat; reduce heat to maintain pressure and cook for 6 minutes. Remove from heat, quickly release pressure, then remove lid. Let cool slightly.

   ELECTRIC: Secure lid. Manually set cooker to 10 minutes and let it come to pressure. Once time is complete, turn off, quickly release pressure, then remove lid. Let cool slightly.

3. Working in batches, purée vegetable mixture, fresh herbs, garlic, 1 teaspoon salt, and ½ teaspoon pepper in a blender, or with an immersion blender, until smooth. Bring to a simmer over medium heat, if using stovetop, or using the sauté function, if using electric. Add butter and stir until melted. Season with salt and pepper, and serve drizzled with cream.

CORN CHOWDER

Corncobs, as well as kernels, are used in the broth for this chowder, drawing on the pressure cooker's ability to concentrate flavors. The result is a soup that tastes like the essence of summer. A bit of curry powder accentuates the sweetness of the corn without offsetting the balance.

―――――――――――――――― SERVES 6 ――――――――――――――――

6 ears corn, shucked

4 tablespoons unsalted butter

2 medium onions, finely chopped

2 garlic cloves, smashed

Coarse salt and freshly ground pepper

1½ teaspoons curry powder

1 quart water

3 fresh bay leaves

2 cups whole milk

Fresh bread, for serving

1. Cut kernels from corncobs and halve cobs; reserve both corncobs and kernels.

2. Melt butter in a 6- to 8-quart stovetop pressure cooker over medium-high heat, or in an electric pressure cooker set to sauté. Add onions, garlic, 2 teaspoons salt, and ¾ teaspoon pepper, and cook, stirring frequently, until onions are translucent, about 5 minutes. Add curry powder and cook, stirring, until fragrant, about 30 seconds. Add the water, reserved corn kernels and cobs, and bay leaves.

3. **STOVETOP:** Secure lid. Bring to high pressure over medium-high heat; reduce heat to maintain pressure and cook for 15 minutes. Remove from heat, quickly release pressure (loosely cover vent with a clean kitchen towel), then remove lid.

   ELECTRIC: Secure lid. Manually set cooker to 15 minutes and let it come to pressure. Once time is complete, turn off, quickly release pressure (loosely cover vent with a clean kitchen towel), then remove lid.

4. Discard corncobs and bay leaves. Stir in milk. Working in batches, purée corn mixture in a blender or with an immersion blender until smooth. Serve immediately, or reheat over medium, if using stovetop, or using the sauté function, if using electric, before serving with bread.

BUTTERY LEEKS WITH CHIVES

The pressure cooker flawlessly replicates the long, slow braising technique of French favorite *les poireaux*. The inherent earthy flavor of the leeks combines beautifully with the sweet braising liquid. Try it served alongside steak with a delicious béarnaise sauce, tossed with pasta and parmesan, or as a mouthwatering filling for a quiche or savory tart.

—————————————————— **SERVES 6** ——————————————————

6 large leeks (white and pale-green parts only), cut lengthwise and rinsed well, then cut crosswise into ½-inch pieces

6 tablespoons unsalted butter

⅓ cup dry white wine

Coarse salt

¼ cup water (for stovetop pressure cooker only)

Snipped fresh chives, for garnish

1. Place leeks, butter, wine, and 1 teaspoon salt In a 6- to 8-quart stovetop or electric pressure cooker. If using stovetop, add the water.

2. **STOVETOP:** Secure lid. Bring to high pressure over medium-high heat; reduce heat to maintain pressure and cook for 2 minutes. Remove from heat, quickly release pressure, then remove lid.

   ELECTRIC: Secure lid. Manually set cooker to 2 minutes and let it come to pressure. Once time is complete, turn off, quickly release pressure, then remove lid.

3. Transfer to a serving dish, top with chives, and serve.

FENNEL WITH OLIVES AND LEMON

Slow-cooking vegetables in olive oil is a classic technique in Mediterranean cuisine—in the pressure cooker, these braised vegetables are ready in under 10 minutes. They're a great make-ahead dish, as they are typically served at room temperature, and are a perfect side for a roasted cut of meat or fish.

SERVES 6

⅔ cup extra-virgin olive oil

2 medium onions, halved lengthwise and thinly sliced

3 large fennel bulbs, tops trimmed and halved lengthwise

⅔ or 1 cup dry white wine

½ cup mixed olives, pitted

6 to 8 mixed herb sprigs, such as rosemary, marjoram, oregano, and savory

Zest of 1 lemon, removed in wide strips with a vegetable peeler

Coarse salt and freshly ground pepper

1. Heat oil in a 6- to 8-quart stovetop pressure cooker over medium-high, or in an electric pressure cooker set to sauté. Add onions and cook, stirring, until translucent, about 5 minutes. Add fennel, wine (1 cup for stovetop; ⅔ cup for electric), olives, herb sprigs, lemon zest, 1 teaspoon salt, and ½ teaspoon pepper.

2. **STOVETOP:** Secure lid. Bring to high pressure over medium-high heat; reduce heat to maintain pressure and cook for 6 minutes. Remove from heat, quickly release pressure, then remove lid.

   ELECTRIC: Secure lid. Manually set cooker to 8 minutes and let it come to pressure. Once time is complete, turn off, quickly release pressure, then remove lid.

3. Transfer to a serving dish and serve warm or at room temperature.

SICILIAN SWISS CHARD WITH TOMATOES

Leafy greens cook in minutes in the machine—about 2 minutes for tender Swiss chard and spinach, 5 or so for sturdier greens such as kale and collards. Just make sure not to overpack them in the cooker (see below).

SERVES 6

¼ cup extra-virgin olive oil

6 large garlic cloves, coarsely chopped

2 bunches (I pound total) Swiss chard, trimmed and sliced into I-inch pieces

I can (14.5 ounces) diced tomatoes

½ cup raisins

¼ teaspoon red-pepper flakes

Coarse salt and freshly ground pepper

1. Heat oil in a 6- to 8-quart stovetop pressure cooker over medium-high, or in an electric pressure cooker set to sauté. Cook garlic, stirring, until golden, about 2 minutes. Add chard, tomatoes (with their juices), raisins, red-pepper flakes, I teaspoon salt, and ½ teaspoon pepper.

2. **STOVETOP:** Secure lid. Bring to high pressure over medium-high heat; reduce heat to maintain pressure and cook for 2 minutes. Remove from heat, quickly release pressure, then remove lid.

   ELECTRIC: Secure lid. Manually set cooker to 2 minutes and let it come to pressure. Once time is complete, turn off, quickly release pressure, then remove lid.

3. Transfer to a serving dish and serve warm or at room temperature.

When dealing with **LEAFY GREENS** in the pressure cooker, take care that the volume does not exceed your cooker's maximum capacity. Fortunately, greens can be easily compressed: Simply use a metal spatula or pot lid to push them down. If they spring back, use a metal insert, steamer basket, or silicone lid to keep them tamed during the cooking process.

ARTICHOKES WITH PROVENÇAL STUFFING

On the stovetop, whole artichokes cook to tender perfection in an hour; in the pressure cooker, the same process takes half the time. Feel free to vary the stuffing (by adding up to ⅓ cup finely grated Parmigiano-Reggiano or Pecorino Romano cheese) and cooking liquids (by using chicken or vegetable stock).

SERVES 4

FOR THE STUFFING

- 2 cups coarse fresh white breadcrumbs
- ½ cup chopped fresh flat-leaf parsley
- ¼ cup finely chopped olives, preferably Niçoise
- 3 tablespoons minced garlic
- ¼ cup extra-virgin olive oil
- Coarse salt and freshly ground pepper

FOR THE ARTICHOKES

- 1 lemon, halved
- 4 globe artichokes
- 1 cup water
- 1 cup dry white wine
- 1 cup puréed tomatoes
- ¼ cup extra-virgin olive oil
- ½ tablespoon minced garlic
- Coarse salt and freshly ground pepper

1. **MAKE THE STUFFING:** Preheat oven to 350°F. Spread breadcrumbs in an even layer on a rimmed baking sheet and toast, stirring once or twice, until pale golden, about 10 minutes. In a bowl, toss breadcrumbs with parsley, olives, garlic, oil, and 1 teaspoon each salt and pepper.

2. **MAKE THE ARTICHOKES:** Squeeze 1 lemon half into a large bowl of cold water. Strip away tough outer leaves from artichokes. Trim stems and top inch of globe. As each one is trimmed, transfer to lemon water to prevent discoloration.

3. Working with one artichoke at a time, loosen leaves and spread away from center. Pull out purple leaves and enough yellow ones to expose fuzzy choke. Scoop out choke with a small spoon, and squeeze juice from remaining lemon half into cavity.

4. Spoon about 2 tablespoons stuffing into cavity of each artichoke. Starting with bottom leaves and spreading leaves open, spoon stuffing between each leaf.

5. In a 6- to 8-quart pressure cooker, combine the water, wine, tomatoes, oil, garlic, ½ teaspoon salt, and ¼ teaspoon pepper. Stand 3 artichokes in liquid, nestling remaining one on top.

6. **STOVETOP:** Secure lid. Bring to high pressure over medium-high heat; reduce heat to maintain pressure and cook for 12 minutes. Remove from heat, quickly release pressure, then remove lid.

   ELECTRIC: Secure lid. Manually set cooker to 15 minutes and let it come to pressure. Once time is complete, turn off, quickly release pressure, then remove lid.

7. Using tongs, transfer artichokes to shallow bowls. Spoon cooking liquid around them and serve.

PART THREE

Sweets & Extras

The best pressure-cooked desserts are those you might expect: steamed sweets and custards (including flan and crème brûlée; the Espresso Crème Brûlée on page 233 is a must) and anything that takes well to the moist heat of the machine. Accordingly, you'll find a couple of puddings in this collection of pressure-cooker sweets, such as a Saffron-Cardamom Tapioca Pudding (page 230) and a Coconut Black Rice Pudding with Mango (page 234), plus a beloved English holiday dessert—fruit-studded plum pudding served with brandy butter. The pressure-cooked cakes we like best are those that are dense and custardy in texture, adorned with little more than a dusting of confectioners' sugar, a dollop of whipped cream, or a glaze of ganache. The machine can also preserve bright, fresh flavors while cutting down on prep time, as is the case with ripe peaches lightly poached in a mint-infused syrup. Served alongside a scoop of vanilla ice cream, they make for an elegant dinner-party dessert with little effort. We also like using the machine to make Candied Citrus Zest (page 243), a holiday favorite: Garnish desserts with it or enjoy it as a snack all year long. Ultimately, desserts in the pressure cooker may be more unexpected than you thought.

DARK CHOCOLATE CAKE

The incredible moistness of this dark chocolate cake may be reason enough to make it. It's also the answer to dessert lovers' prayers in summer, when you can't even think about turning the oven on. If the batter is not yet set in the middle after the recommended time, bring the pressure cooker back to pressure and cook for an additional 5 minutes. We kept the topping light here, with a sprinkling of confectioners' sugar—and then couldn't resist adding some whipped cream and fresh berries on the side. For an extra dose of chocolate, glaze the cake with a silky ganache (page 222) before serving.

SERVES 6

Unsalted butter, for pan

1¼ cups all-purpose flour

¾ cup dark brown sugar

½ cup Dutch-process cocoa powder

1 teaspoon baking powder

½ teaspoon baking soda

Coarse salt

5 cups water

½ cup vegetable oil

2 large eggs

1 tablespoon confectioners' sugar (optional)

Whipped Cream, for serving (page 222, optional)

Chocolate Ganache (page 222, optional)

1. Make a foil sling for the pressure cooker (see page 18). Butter a 7-inch cake pan or cake pan insert for pressure cooker. Line with parchment round and butter parchment.

2. In a medium bowl, whisk together flour, brown sugar, cocoa, baking powder, baking soda, and ¾ teaspoon salt. In another bowl, whisk together 1 cup water, the oil, and eggs. Whisk flour mixture into egg mixture. Pour batter into prepared pan and cover with aluminum foil.

3. Pour remaining 4 cups water into a 6- to 8-quart pressure cooker; set a 1-inch rack on bottom. Arrange foil sling under cake pan and set cake on top of rack.

4. **STOVETOP:** Secure lid. Bring to high pressure over medium-high heat; reduce heat to maintain pressure and cook for 25 minutes. Remove from heat, quickly release pressure, then remove lid.

   ELECTRIC: Secure lid. Manually set cooker to 33 minutes and let it come to pressure. Once time is complete, turn off, quickly release pressure, then remove lid.

5. Use sling to remove cake from pressure cooker and remove foil. Run a knife around edge of cake to loosen, then invert cake onto a serving plate. Remove parchment and transfer to a wire rack to cool slightly. Dust with confectioners' sugar and serve with whipped cream, if desired; or glaze with ganache. Serve warm or at room temperature.

recipe continues

WHIPPED CREAM

1 cup cold heavy cream

2 tablespoons confectioners' sugar (optional)

Using a mixer or by hand, whisk cream in a well-chilled bowl until soft peaks form. Add sugar, as desired (or omit, for unsweetened whipped cream), and whisk until medium-stiff peaks form.

CHOCOLATE GANACHE

8 ounces semisweet chocolate

1 cup heavy cream

⅛ teaspoon coarse salt

1. Coarsely chop chocolate.

2. Bring cream just to a boil over medium-high heat. Pour over chocolate, and add salt. Let stand for 10 minutes (don't stir, as doing so will cool the ganache too quickly, making it grainy).

3. Stir with a whisk until smooth and shiny, to break up any pieces.

4. To glaze, set room-temperature cake on a wire rack over a baking sheet. Pour warm ganache over cake.

MARTHA'S ENGLISH PLUM PUDDING

4 ounces (about ½ cup) cold beef suet or unsalted butter, grated or finely chopped, plus more for mold

¼ cup all-purpose flour

¼ cup dark brown sugar

1 teaspoon freshly grated nutmeg

½ teaspoon ground cinnamon

½ teaspoon ground mace

¼ teaspoon ground allspice

Coarse salt

½ cup dark raisins

½ cup golden raisins

½ cup dried currants

1 tablespoon finely grated orange zest

2 large eggs, separated

½ cup brandy, plus more for dousing and flambéing

1 cup fresh breadcrumbs

2 quarts boiling water

Brandy Butter (page 225)

After many a Christmas Eve dinner, Martha brought this classic dessert, aflame with brandy, to her holiday table. Studded with dried fruits and nicely spiced, plum pudding is customarily made months ahead. Traditionally the pudding takes about 8 hours to steam, but the pressure cooker achieves the same result in 90 minutes or less. Suet is the fat of choice, since it keeps indefinitely at room temperature. (Unsalted butter is a fine substitute, but only if you're serving the pudding right away.) Serve with Brandy Butter (page 225)

—————————— **SERVES 6 TO 8** ——————————

1. Grease a 1-quart heatproof mold, such as a 6- to 7-inch ceramic bowl that will fit easily inside the pressure cooker. Make a foil sling for the pressure cooker (see page 18).

2. In a small bowl, combine flour, brown sugar, nutmeg, cinnamon, mace, allspice, and ¼ teaspoon salt. In a large bowl, combine suet, raisins, currants, and zest. Add flour mixture to fruit mixture, using your hands to coat dried fruit and suet. In another bowl, beat together egg yolks, brandy, and breadcrumbs; stir into fruit mixture to combine.

3. With a mixer on medium-high, beat egg whites just until firm peaks form; fold into fruit batter.

4. Pour batter into prepared mold. Cover top with a 10-inch circle of parchment, then cover tightly with aluminum foil; tie a string under lip of bowl to seal. Place a 1-inch-high rack in a 6- to 8-quart pressure cooker, and add the boiling water. Arrange foil sling under bowl and set bowl on top of rack.

5. **STOVETOP:** Secure lid. Bring to high pressure over medium-high heat; reduce heat to maintain pressure and cook for 75 minutes. Remove from heat, quickly release pressure, then remove lid.

   ELECTRIC: Secure lid. Manually set cooker to 90 minutes and let it come to pressure. Once time is complete, turn off, quickly release pressure, then remove lid.

recipe continues

6. Use sling to remove bowl from pressure cooker and remove foil and parchment. Let stand 5 minutes, then invert onto a small cake plate. To flambé: Heat 2 tablespoons brandy in a small pot. Using a long fireplace match or butane lighter, ignite brandy. Carefully pour over pudding and bring to table flaming. Cut into 8 wedges and serve with Brandy Butter (recipe below).

If keeping the pudding for weeks or months, up to 1 year: Store in bowl at cool room temperature covered with parchment-lined foil and douse every week or so with 2 tablespoons brandy.

1. **TO REHEAT AND SERVE:** Cover bowl again with parchment-lined foil and tie around lip with string. Add 1 quart water to a 6- to 8-quart pressure cooker. Arrange foil sling under bowl and set bowl on top of rack.

2. **STOVETOP:** Secure lid. Bring to high pressure over medium-high heat; reduce heat to maintain pressure and cook for 15 minutes. Remove from heat, quickly release pressure, then remove lid.

   ELECTRIC: Secure lid. Manually set cooker to 15 minutes and let it come to pressure. Once time is complete, turn off, quickly release pressure, then remove lid.

3. Use sling to remove bowl from pressure cooker and remove foil. Invert onto a small cake plate. Heat 2 tablespoons brandy in a small pot. Using a long fireplace match or butane lighter, ignite brandy. Carefully pour over pudding and bring to table flaming. Cut into 8 wedges and serve with brandy butter.

BRANDY BUTTER

—————————— MAKES ABOUT 1 CUP ——————————

1 stick (½ cup) unsalted butter, softened	2 cups confectioners' sugar	¼ cup brandy Coarse salt

With a mixer on medium, beat butter until creamy, about 2 minutes. Add half the confectioners' sugar and beat until smooth, about 30 seconds. Add brandy, a little at a time, while beating. Add remaining confectioners' sugar and ½ teaspoon salt and beat until smooth, about 30 seconds more.

RASPBERRY UPSIDE-DOWN CAKE

It's hard to go wrong with an upside-down cake. This one tastes a lot like British steamed puddings such as the Fruit Hat or Spotted Dick, but it is made with fresh fruits instead of dried ones. If you don't have raspberries, try mangoes, strawberries, blueberries, pears, or pineapples. And don't skimp on the softly whipped cream served alongside; spike it with Grand Marnier, if you wish, to highlight the same flavor used in the cake itself.

SERVES 6

I stick (½ cup) unsalted butter, melted and cooled slightly, plus more for pan

½ cup plus 2 tablespoons sugar

12 ounces fresh raspberries, picked over, plus more for serving

I cup all-purpose flour

1¾ teaspoons baking powder

Coarse salt

I large egg

½ cup whole milk

Finely grated zest of I orange

I tablespoon Grand Marnier liqueur

I teaspoon pure vanilla extract

3 cups water

Whipped Cream, for serving (optional, page 222)

1. Make a foil sling for the pressure cooker (see page 18). Butter a 7-inch cake pan or cake pan insert for pressure cooker. Line with parchment round, butter parchment, and sprinkle with 2 tablespoons sugar. Top sugar with an even layer of raspberries.

2. Whisk together flour, baking powder, ½ teaspoon salt, and remaining ½ cup sugar in a bowl. In a large bowl, whisk together egg, milk, butter, zest, Grand Marnier, and vanilla. Whisk flour mixture into egg mixture until just combined. Pour batter over fruit, spreading evenly. Cover pan with aluminum foil.

3. Pour the water into a 6- to 8-quart pressure cooker; set a 1-inch rack on bottom. Arrange foil sling under cake pan and set cake on top of rack.

4. **STOVETOP:** Secure lid. Bring to high pressure over medium-high heat; reduce heat to maintain pressure and cook for 30 minutes. Remove from heat, quickly release pressure, then remove lid.

   ELECTRIC: Secure lid. Manually set cooker to 35 minutes and let it come to pressure. Once time is complete, turn off, quickly release pressure, then remove lid.

5. Use sling to remove cake from pressure cooker and remove foil. Let stand 10 minutes, run a knife around edge of cake to loosen, then invert cake onto a serving plate. Remove parchment and serve topped with berries and whipped cream, if desired.

CINNAMON-CARAMEL FLAN

Flan, like crème brûlée, has a custard base, but it's topped with caramel instead of crisp caramelized sugar. We've added cinnamon to the custard for a lovely, warm flavor. Don't be intimidated to try this delectable dessert—you'll know that it's done when the custard trembles just slightly in the center.

———— SERVES 6 ————

1¼ cups sugar

2 cups plus 3 tablespoons water

4 large eggs

2 cups half-and-half

¾ teaspoon ground cinnamon

Coarse salt

1. Make a foil sling for the pressure cooker (see page 18).

2. Combine ¾ cup sugar and 3 tablespoons water in a tall-sided saucepan. Bring to a boil over medium heat and cook without stirring, swirling saucepan occasionally, until caramel is dark amber in color, about 8 minutes. Immediately pour caramel into a 7-inch cake pan and let cool slightly.

3. Whisk eggs in a medium bowl. Add half-and-half, cinnamon, ½ teaspoon salt, and remaining ½ cup sugar, and whisk until combined. Pour custard over caramel in cake pan and cover pan with aluminum foil.

4. Pour remaining 2 cups water into a 6- to 8-quart pressure cooker; set a 1-inch rack on bottom. Arrange foil sling under cake pan and set pan on top of rack.

5. **STOVETOP:** Secure lid. Bring to high pressure over medium-high heat; reduce heat to maintain pressure and cook for 15 minutes. Remove from heat, quickly release pressure, then remove lid.

   ELECTRIC: Secure lid. Manually set cooker to 7 minutes and let it come to pressure. Once time is complete, turn off and let pressure decrease naturally for 10 minutes. Release remaining pressure, if necessary, then remove lid.

6. Use sling to remove flan from pressure cooker. Reserve caramel. Transfer to a wire rack and let cool completely. Refrigerate until set, at least 2 hours or up to 3 days. To unmold, run a sharp knife carefully around edges of pan. Invert onto a serving plate and serve flan with reserved caramel.

SAFFRON-CARDAMOM TAPIOCA PUDDING

Saffron imparts its beautiful yellow hue to many traditional Persian and Indian desserts, while cardamom lends subtle floral notes. Here, we used both in a tapioca pudding, which cooks at magical speed in the pressure cooker. (It's not necessary to soak the tapioca before cooking, as you would if making it on the stove.) The secret to this pudding is to cook the tapioca first, then add the more heat-sensitive custard ingredients. Checking the temperature of the custard (it should not go above 180°F) with an instant-read thermometer will ensure that it doesn't curdle.

―――――――――――――――― **SERVES 4 TO 6** ――――――――――――――――

1½ or 2 cups water

½ cup small pearl tapioca

½ cup heavy cream

⅓ cup sugar

2 large egg yolks

¼ teaspoon ground cardamom

Small pinch saffron, crumbled

Coarse salt

1. In a 6- to 8-quart pressure cooker, whisk together water (2 cups for stovetop; 1½ cups for electric) and tapioca.

2. **STOVETOP:** Secure lid. Bring to high pressure over medium-high heat; reduce heat to maintain pressure and cook for 6 minutes. Remove from heat and let pressure decrease naturally for 10 minutes. Release remaining pressure, if necessary, then remove lid. Return cooker to medium heat.

   ELECTRIC: Secure lid. Manually set cooker to 6 minutes and let it come to pressure. Once time is complete, let pressure decrease naturally for 10 minutes. Release remaining pressure, if necessary, then remove lid. Set cooker to sauté.

3. Whisk together cream, sugar, egg yolks, cardamom, saffron, and ½ teaspoon salt in a medium bowl. Add cream mixture to pressure cooker, and cook, stirring constantly, until thickened and custard coats the back of a spoon, about 3 minutes.

4. Transfer tapioca pudding to ramekins or small bowls and let cool completely. Cover with plastic wrap and refrigerate until set, at least 3 hours or up to 5 days.

ESPRESSO CRÈME BRÛLÉE

Espresso gives this crème brûlée a dark, earthy undertone, and it's made velvety through the steam of the pressure cooker. Eight small (3-ounce) ramekins can be stacked on a rack and take only 5 minutes to cook under pressure. You'll be left with plenty of time to perform the finishing touch—caramelizing the sugar topping—under the broiler or with a kitchen torch to achieve that crisp topping that contrasts so beautifully with the creamy custard.

SERVES 8

- 2 cups heavy cream
- 2 teaspoons instant espresso powder
- 8 large egg yolks
- ⅓ cup granulated sugar
- 1½ teaspoons pure vanilla extract
- Coarse salt
- 2 cups water
- Superfine sugar, for topping

1. Combine cream and espresso powder in a medium saucepan. Bring to a simmer over medium heat, whisking until powder is dissolved (do not let boil over).

2. Whisk together yolks, granulated sugar, vanilla, and a pinch of salt in a medium bowl. Slowly whisk in hot cream mixture. Divide mixture among 8 small (3-ounce) ramekins and cover each with aluminum foil.

3. Pour the water into a 6- to 8-quart pressure cooker, set a 1-inch-high rack on bottom. Arrange 5 ramekins in a circle on rack and stack remaining 3 on top.

4. **STOVETOP:** Secure lid. Bring to high pressure over medium-high heat; reduce heat to maintain pressure and cook for 4 minutes. Remove from heat, quickly release pressure, then remove lid.

   ELECTRIC: Secure lid. Manually set cooker to 5 minutes and let it come to pressure. Once time is complete, turn off, quickly release pressure, then remove lid.

5. Transfer ramekins to a tray and let cool completely. Cover with plastic wrap and refrigerate until set, at least 1 hour or up to 1 week.

6. Just before serving, heat broiler with rack about 4 inches from heating element. Sprinkle about 1 teaspoon superfine sugar evenly over each custard. Place under broiler until sugar bubbles and turns amber, 3 to 5 minutes. (Alternatively, caramelize tops of custards with a kitchen torch.) Serve immediately.

COCONUT BLACK RICE PUDDING WITH MANGO

In Imperial China, black rice—also called forbidden or emperor's rice—was quite rare and therefore prized. Today it can be found at gourmet grocers and online, but it's no less appreciated for its chewy texture and slight nuttiness. A richer rice pudding than one made with white rice, this mango and coconut version has a tropical feel—it's the perfect sour-sweet-creamy dessert to serve after a meal of jerk chicken or Caribbean fish stew. We used brown sugar for a stronger flavor; an unrefined palm sugar would be even better.

SERVES 6

2 cups black rice

2 cans (14 ounces each) unsweetened coconut milk

1¼ or 1¾ cups water

¾ cup dark brown sugar

Coarse salt

2 ripe mangoes, peeled, pitted, and diced

1. In a 6- to 8-quart pressure cooker, combine rice, coconut milk, water (1¾ cups for stovetop; 1¼ cups for electric), brown sugar, and ¼ teaspoon salt.

2. **STOVETOP:** Secure lid. Bring to high pressure over medium-high heat; reduce heat to maintain pressure and cook for 25 minutes. Remove from heat, quickly release pressure, then remove lid.

   ELECTRIC: Secure lid. Manually set cooker to 30 minutes and let it come to pressure. Once time is complete, turn off, quickly release pressure, then remove lid.

3. Serve warm or at room temperature, topped with mangoes.

APRICOT-AND-PRUNE COMPOTE WITH PORT

A versatile compote makes serving dessert especially easy, even on a weeknight. In the pressure cooker, dried fruit becomes very tender as it absorbs the deep notes of whatever liquid you're using to poach it—in this case, port. Serve it over mascarpone, as we did, ice cream (our favorites are ginger or classic vanilla), or slices of pound cake. Feel free to try other combinations of fruit and wine, such as prunes and figs with red wine, or apricots, raisins, and cherries with white wine—just maintain the proportions here.

—————————————— SERVES 4 ——————————————

1 cup dried apricots

1 cup pitted prunes

Finely grated zest and fresh juice of 2 oranges (about ¾ cup)

1 cup port wine

½ cup sugar

Coarse salt

1 vanilla bean, split

Mascarpone, for serving (optional)

1. In a 6- to 8-quart pressure cooker, combine apricots, prunes, orange zest and juice, port, sugar, and a pinch of salt. Using the dull side of a paring knife, scrape seeds from vanilla bean into pressure cooker, then add bean.

2. **STOVETOP:** Secure lid. Bring to high pressure over medium-high heat; reduce heat to maintain pressure and cook for 4 minutes. Remove from heat, quickly release pressure, then remove lid. (Discard vanilla bean.)

   ELECTRIC: Secure lid. Manually set cooker to 6 minutes and let it come to pressure. Once time is complete, turn off, quickly release pressure, then remove lid. (Discard vanilla bean.)

3. Serve compote warm or at room temperature with a dollop of mascarpone, if desired.

POACHED PEACHES WITH MINT

There's little that can compete with a perfectly ripe fresh peach. But poached peaches come close, especially when instantly infused with vanilla and mint. Make sure to choose peaches that yield gently to the touch but are not too soft. You want them at just the right stage of ripeness so they will hold up under pressure.

SERVES 4

- 4 firm, ripe peaches
- 4 cups water
- 1 small bunch fresh mint, plus a few sprigs for garnish
- 1 cup sugar
- 1 vanilla bean, split

1. Lightly score the bottom of each peach with an X. In a 6- to 8-quart pressure cooker, combine peaches, the water, mint, and sugar. Using the dull side of a paring knife, scrape seeds from vanilla beans into pressure cooker, then add bean.

2. **STOVETOP:** Secure lid. Bring to high pressure over medium-high heat; reduce heat to maintain pressure and cook, 1 minute for softer peaches, 2 minutes for firm peaches. Remove from heat, quickly release pressure, and remove lid.

   ELECTRIC: Secure lid. Manually set cooker to 2 minutes and let it come to pressure. Once time is complete, turn off, quickly release pressure, then remove lid.

3. With a slotted spoon, transfer peaches to a bowl and let cool slightly. (Discard mint sprigs and vanilla bean.) Using a paring knife, peel peaches. Serve peaches with syrup and a sprig of mint.

CANDIED CITRUS ZEST

From the earliest days of *Martha Stewart Living*, our test kitchen cooks and editors have been fans of candied citrus zest at holiday time—using it to adorn countless cakes, pies, puddings, and cookies. Imagine our delight when we discovered how quickly and easily we could prepare a batch in the pressure cooker. Add it to your favorite confection or package it into small boxes for gift giving. Holiday prep time just got a lot shorter, and sweeter.

— MAKES ABOUT 3 CUPS —

6 navel oranges, preferably organic

5½ or 6 cups water

1½ cups sugar

Coarse salt

1. Using a vegetable peeler, remove zest from oranges in wide strips. Remove white pith using a sharp knife. Cut zest into thin strips.

2. Heat the orange zest and 4 cups water in a 6- to 8-quart stovetop pressure cooker over medium-high heat, or in an electric pressure cooker set to sauté. Bring to a boil and cook, uncovered, until softened, about 5 minutes.

3. Strain zest through a fine-mesh sieve set over a large bowl and return to cooker with remaining water (2 cups for stovetop; 1½ cups for electric), the sugar, and ½ teaspoon salt.

4. **STOVETOP:** Secure lid. Bring to high pressure over medium-high heat; reduce heat to maintain pressure and cook for 12 minutes. Remove from heat, quickly release pressure, then remove lid.

   ELECTRIC: Secure lid. Manually set cooker to 15 minutes and let it come to pressure. Once time is complete, turn off, quickly release pressure, then remove lid.

5. Allow to cool completely. (Store candied orange zest with syrup in an airtight container in the refrigerator for up to 1 month.)

ACKNOWLEDGMENTS

Led by the editorial team of Ellen Morrissey, Susanne Ruppert, Bridget Fitzgerald, and Nanette Maxim, our ninety-first book was the collaboration of many talented individuals who contributed their vast knowledge, considerable time, and endless generosity, including Kevin Sharkey, who so kindly lent his creative guidance.

Thank you to everyone in the Martha Stewart Living kitchen for their invaluable culinary expertise, but especially to Thomas Joseph, Sarah Carey, Greg Lofts, and Kavita Thirupu-vanam for helping us to always put our readers first. Shelley Wiseman and Ian Knauer, in particular, were instrumental in showing us the pressure cooker's endless delicious possibilities.

Marcus Nilsson, James Dunlinson, Frances Boswell, and Alistair Turnbull transformed each recipe into a stunning image, with their keen photography, art direction, and styling that graces every page.

Other key players include: Ian Baguskas, Jenny Comita, Denise Ginley, Emerald Layne, Sanaë Lemoine, Josefa Palacios, Grace Parisi, Gertrude Porter, Katie Stilo, Stacey Tyrell, and Mike Varrassi.

We are especially thankful to our Potter family, who has supported us each step of the way: Jennifer Sit, Jen Wang, Linnea Knollmueller, Neil Spitkovsky, Mark McCauslin, Amy Boorstein, Marysarah Quinn, Aaron Wehner, Doris Cooper, Maya Mavjee, Kate Tyler, Jana Branson, and Stephanie Davis.

INDEX

Published in the United States by Clarkson Potter/Publishers,
an imprint of the Crown Publishing Group, a division of
Penguin Random House LLC, New York.
clarksonpotter.com
marthastewart.com

CLARKSON POTTER is a trademark and
POTTER with colophon is a registered trademark of
Penguin Random House LLC.

Library of Congress Cataloging-in-Publication Data
Names: Stewart, Martha. | Martha Stewart Living.
Title: Martha Stewart's pressure cooker: 100+ fabulous new
    recipes for the pressure cooker, multicooker,
    and Instant Pot® / editors of Martha Stewart Living.
Other titles: Martha Stewart Living.
Description: First edition. | New York : Clarkson Potter/
    Publishers, 2018.
Identifiers: LCCN 2017050562 | ISBN 9781524763350 (pbk.) |
    ISBN 9781524763367 (ebook)
Subjects: LCSH: Pressure cooking. | LCGFT: Cookbooks.
Classification: LCC TX840.P7 M37 2018 |
    DDC 641.5/87—dc23
LC record available at https://lccn.loc.gov/2017050562

ISBN 978-1-5247-6335-0
Ebook ISBN 978-1-5247-6336-7

Printed in China

Book and cover design by Jen Wang
Book and cover photographs by Marcus Nilsson

10 9 8 7 6 5 4 3 2 1

First Edition